For the Death of Dustin Essary
a music novel

by
Tim McDonald

Wordvendor Publishing

Copyright © 2015 by Tim McDonald
All rights reserved

Edited by Rosa Cays

Book design by Cindy Hayton

Cover art by Svetlana Antropova
The Old Neighborhood (2015), 28 x 22 inches. Oil on canvas.

© All song lyrics written by Tim McDonald
Broken Poets / Wordvendor Music ASCAP

www.amusicnovel.com
www.brokenpoets.com

ISBN: 978-0-692-60523-3

Author's Note

The first edition of this book will always remain online, where the songs can be listened to in certain parts of the story and the lyrics can be read as you go along. It's why I subtitled it "a music novel." I'm happy to release this printed version, though, including the song lyrics, which still help to carry the idea I had in mind. For the full experience, you can always go to:

www.amusicnovel.com

"Tim McDonald has written a tale of awkward youth and death too young, and he has told it with his music and lyrics integrated into the story. The experience of reading lyrics while listening to the music, knowing I was still inside the story, was unique and memorable. His writing style gets uncomfortably close to the true nature of his 7th grade main character (a very close version of Tim as a kid). This was annoying at first—I wanted to tell him to stop getting distracted by everything—but then I recalled my own behavior in junior high. My favorite chapter was the one that centered on his adventures with the homeless man, Pat. The professional writer in me is dying to adapt it into a marvelous short film or one-act play. It's moving, tough, and insightful. Red Barber, the great sports writer, said, "Writing is easy. Just sit down and open a vein." In Tim McDonald's debut novel, *For the Death of Dustin Essary*, you'll feel the blood of his heart and soul everywhere. McDonald's story does well to honor his childhood friend."

—Joey Robert Parks,
 Ghostwriter & author

For the Death of Dustin Essary
a music novel

Prologue
April 27, 2015

I tried telling this story to the cops once but I still got arrested. It was the drunk and mysterious version that first came to mind when I was digging in my wallet for my license but found Dustin's old memorial service thing instead.

"HE WAS MY BEST FRIEND, YA' KNOW ... DUSTIN ESSRY... HE WAS ONLY 13 WHEN HE DIED, TOO ... LEG BONE CANCER ... HE'S WHY I STARTED DOIN' MUSIC, THOUGH—"

"STEP OUT OF THE CAR, SIR."

"AND THOSE DREAMS HE HAD ... LIKE HE KNEW IT ALL SOMEHOW ... BEFORE HE DIED, I MEAN ... SEPTEMPER TWENY SEVEN, NINETEEN SEVNY EIGHT."

And not that what I was saying had anything to do with me being wasted or even waiting at the light for too long, which is why they pulled me over in the first place. But what happened with Dustin was my big excuse back then, so I was hoping they'd feel sorry for me and let me off, I guess.

Dustin was just a better person, though. And I don't just mean it in the usual way—like he was the nicest guy you ever want to meet or something; even though he was, actually. But he was just one of those people where you know they're for real right up front ... like genuine. Selfless. And that's the one thing that's bothered me ever since—the fact that you meet people all the time who might deserve it. The kind that live on for years with all their selfish bullshit. *Jesus*, I'm probably one of them. But then someone like Dustin gets taken away early. It just doesn't make any sense.

So I've started to think that what he told me before he died might have actually happened, about the strange dreams he said he had and everything he described to me after that. And yeah, I still feel guilty since at the time I never believed him.

But with those song lyrics that came to me recently, the ones so similar to what he told me back then, along with all the songs I've written through the years that always lead back to me dealing with Dustin's death to begin with ... Well, the more I go over it in my mind, the more I see a connection.

And it's not like I believe in that old bullshit adage, that *everything happens for a reason*, because it doesn't. But when certain things line up like this, the kind of things too personal for it to be just random, well, *that's* when it makes you wonder. Had you asked me back then, though, I might have told you a whole different story …

To Dream of Another Life

The dreams that will come to you
 when you're wide open
To let them into your mind
 happens more oftentimes
Not while you're waiting,
 no not while you're waiting for anything
And we've all got a story
 of some happy ending
Like the man who lived next to
 the man who lost everything
And outside these games we play,
 does losing or winning mean anything

And the sun shines today
And God is in the garden
As I lie awake and dream of another life

Back in 1718 I lost all my hope then
I was drowned in this river
 and brought back to life again
For all I know now I will die on the day
 I find hope again
Because the devil here worships

just one man's religion
With a shadow cast over
the light that may reach him
You show me an angel
and I'll show you a devil that follows him

And the sun shines today
And God is in the garden
As I lie awake and dream of another life

And above the door I found
keys that were left behind
To hold back the fear
that I've locked myself in behind
And outside this room I will find some new fear
I can hide behind
If we all started over with just one new decision
That was made for the sake of
or in spite of my living here
And for all I know now I will question the truth
From the meaning I've found
for all that I can do

When the sun shines today
And God is in the garden
As I lie awake and dream of another life

I
March 1980

So I guess I'm supposed to tell you what happened a few years ago, around the time before Dustin died. That was the older version of me talking before, by the way, so you can probably tell everything I ended up thinking was pretty stupid. I mean, I could hardly understand all the dream crap when it happened so I'm not sure what he meant, really. But I just figure I'll tell you my side so you know the truth at least. That stuff about me writing songs later was kind of cool, though, I guess.

Anyway, all I know at this point is that I still miss Dustin a lot, and I wish my parents would have never moved us out here to Bumfuck Egypt Apache Junction since it sucks so bad. Phoenix was the best, though, and that's where we were living at the time, so I should probably just tell you about that first.

It was just better there, I think. Like maybe how it feels if you're living near the ocean, just with a bunch of huge rocks instead. Like wherever you were at, you could see Camelback Mountain. Or just "the mountain" is what we called it. We lived right there at the face of it, too. Not in the rich neighborhoods, but down around 44th and Camelback, which was where everything happened most of the time anyway.

It was the perfect corner, though. There was a Circle K with a liquor store right next to it; a Shell station across from that with a cigarette machine outside so you could get smokes if you wanted; a Jack in the Crack, a little park to hang out in, and even a back alley that ran behind the park fence for a perfect escape route. I mean, what more could a little 13-year-old asshole need? Actually, I wasn't a complete asshole yet, but I'll just tell you about all that later. We were still bored, though—just like here in the Junction. I hear it's boring no matter where you're at, though, really.

Anyway, it was on that Saturday, sometime around that last April before Dustin died when he first brought it up, about all the dream crap, I mean. I remember it rained for like two days straight right before that, too, so when it finally started to clear up we couldn't wait to get out. Dustin came by my house around noon, and since his parents had let him out, my mom gave in pretty quick.

"Okay, but only for a while—and no bikes," she said.

"Just going up to Circle K to mess around!" I yelled, halfway out the front door already.

But Dustin had just told me about a flash flood that tore up one of the roads up near the mountain so our plan was to go check it out. My older brother was out front smoking a cigarette when we left, though.

"*Liar*," he said.

"Shut up, Mike," I muttered, as me and Dustin started walking up the sidewalk.

"WHAT?" he yelled, and it looked like he might come after us, so we took off running at that point and I could still hear him yelling some stuff as we made it to the alley at the end of the street. Something about me being a little shithead, but I couldn't make out the rest.

"My brother does the same thing," Dustin said. "It's like he knows when I'm lying or something. He's like one of those Santa's helpers." He laughed.

"Yeah, mine's like a fucking Kris Kringle." I was convinced my brother had special powers at that point. Then Dustin started singing that "Santa Claus is Coming to Town" song, and just making stuff up as he went.

"*Wait*. He knows when you're a shithead, he knows when you're a fake, you know he's still a jackass, so you better be good for that ol' fucker's sake ..."

It was pretty funny, though, so we both took turns trading off verses about each other's brother as we made our way up the alley till we finally got bored with it.

I needed to stop by Circle K first so I could at least say I went there, but when we got to the corner there was an ambulance parked out in front of the liquor store with a bunch of people around. We pushed our way through the crowd to try to see what had happened, and after a while they wheeled some old guy out on a stretcher with one of those masks on his face.

"Heart attack," the lady said next to us.

Jesus, I thought.

But then the paramedics were just standing there, not even helping the guy, so we kind of got bored just waiting around. So we went over to Circle, got a couple of Freezies, checked the payphones for change, and then went back again to see if anything had happened. The paramedics were still standing there, but now the cops were there asking the liquor store guy a bunch of questions.

While we were waiting, I took a couple big drinks off my Freezie and then realized I went too far. I knew there was nothing I could do about it either, so I just stood there with my head down.

"Ahhhhhhh!" I yelled.

"What?" Dustin asked, since people were looking at us.

"Ahhhhhhh! Ahhhhhhh!" I kept yelling, but I couldn't help it, really.

"Seriously, what's wrong?" Dustin asked again.

"*Freeze ache*," I said finally, as the pain started to fade. I was afraid to even take another drink so I just threw it out.

And then they were loading the guy in the ambulance so we decided to start heading up towards the mountain after that. We checked the smoke machine at the gas station before we left, but there were way too many people around to try and buy any, let alone stick your arm up inside if you wanted to steal a pack. So we headed out to the corner and as we were waiting to cross Camelback Road, we could see the ambulance pulling out of the parking lot.

"No sirens," Dustin said. "Means the guy didn't make it."

And I thought he was joking at first, but then he looked all serious, and I heard it was true later, too—that if somebody dies before they get to the hospital they don't even bother running the sirens anymore, I guess. It was just weird, though, since Dustin was the one that told me about it.

Anyway, as we were walking up 44th, it looked like it was going to rain again, probably, but we were pretty sure we could make it there and back before it got too bad. There was still a bunch of water along the road, though, so for every car that passed we had to worry if some asshole was going to try to spray us.

Dustin's brother had told him that it was Solano Drive that got washed out up near Echo Canyon, so we decided to cut up through the Canyon Estates to try to get there faster. It always felt weird in those rich neighborhoods, though, like people were staring out the windows at us, so instead of feeling weird about it we just jumped someone's fence and started hiking up a wash that was going in the same direction.

You could see how the flood really ripped through there, too. There were all sorts of cactus torn up, and a bunch of sand and broken trees piled up everywhere. And it even started to rain a little while we were down there, and all I could think of was another flash flood coming through at any second. Dustin said it had to rain a lot harder for it to happen, though, and I knew he was right, probably, but still.

But we hiked up the wash as far as we could, even though when we climbed up the bank at the end we were still pretty far from Echo Canyon. We were right there close to the mountain after that, though, and it was just hard to believe how big it was, really. I mean, even the boulders down closer to us were as big as mine or Dustin's house, probably. And with that huge rock face shooting up into the sky like that, and with the clouds coming in around it and everything—it was pretty awesome.

But that's when we were just standing there in that desert field above the wash, just checking everything out for a minute.

"We're way off from Solano Drive," I said as I threw a rock in the other direction.

Dustin looked up as it started to rain a little harder. "We should probably get back," he said.

And then I chucked another rock and it kind of flew past Dustin's head by accident, but that's when it started pouring like crazy, so we ran for cover under the big eucalyptus trees that were lined up along the wash. There were some bigger ones towards the middle with the roots all bunched together so we found a place to stay dry there, no problem.

"Shouldn't throw stuff," Dustin said as we got in out of the rain, brushing off our hair and our jackets. I told him I was sorry but he still seemed kind of pissed.

There was a bunch of garbage and cigarette butts laying under the trees, like maybe somebody had a fort there at some point, and it looked like the water had flooded up over the bank the day before, too. Dustin found a scrap of paper and showed me where you could kind of see half a naked lady with some writing underneath.

"She wasn't used ... to ... being with ... men who ..." he read over the sound of the rain.

"*Jesus,*" I said, trying to imagine what else might have been there.

But then the rain started coming down even harder after that, and the wind was blowing like crazy all of a sudden, so we just sat up against one of the big trees in the middle and tried to stay dry.

I kept noticing all the cigarette butts laying around, thinking of the half pack of Dorals I had stashed in the brick fence in our side yard, the ones I couldn't get to since my stupid brother was there when we left.

But that's when Dustin got up all of a sudden and walked out to where the rain was coming down and just stood there looking out at the wash. And I guess it was kind of weird since he wasn't saying anything at first, but I wasn't really paying attention either, and then he just started telling me this stuff.

"You ever have a dream where people are talking?" he asked.

"What, like a nightmare?" I said, thinking it was funny, but then I remembered all the bad dreams I was having a few years before that, so I felt kind of weird after I said it.

Dustin looked back and seemed excited.

"No, it wasn't like that," he said, "but everything seemed so real, so I was kind of scared I was awake at first. But it was like I was standing on the side of this mountain," he explained, "and you could see the ocean down below. And there were these huge trees all around—a *lot* bigger than these," he said, looking up, "but then we were just standing there, watching these big waves coming in and—"

"Who?" I asked.

"And there were these weird-looking plants everywhere, too, like all different colors ... but they weren't like flowers—"

"Who was there, though?" I asked again, and I was getting kind of irritated since the whole thing just sounded stupid.

"Okay, yeah, I was just going to say, there was this old guy there, kind of like a scientist, or an inventor, maybe. At least it seemed like it from all the stuff he was saying."

I scoffed. "It wasn't *Greenwald*, was it?" Greenwald was this seventh grade science teacher we had who was a real asshole, and especially to me for some reason.

Dustin gave me a disgusted look. "No, it wasn't him," he said. "It was just weird, though. I mean, he wasn't like a normal person."

The rain was still coming down pretty hard and you could see the wash had started to flood down below us. Dustin came back and sat down next to me, wiping his face with the inside of his jacket.

"Really, though," he said, "and it was like I was awake the whole time, too ... just like we're sitting here. And then the guy just started telling me this stuff." Dustin shook his head.

I rubbed my face a little so he couldn't see me laughing, but I guess he could tell anyway.

"What, you don't believe me?" he asked.

"No, I do. I just ... I mean, I believe you." I said. But I didn't really.

Dustin gave me this irritated look and then leaned back and pulled this folded-up yellow piece of paper from his front pocket.

"I'm serious, though," he said, "I even wrote a lot of it down so I could remember."

"Let me see it," I said as I tried to grab it from him, but he pulled it away too fast. I could see some stuff written though, and some weird-looking drawings he had scratched in blue ink as he flattened the sheet out against his knee.

"I had the same dream a couple times now," Dustin said, "and every time the guy kind of says the same thing, just in a different way, I guess. And it's not like I even know what it's about, really. I mean, I do ... I mean, I understand, I think. But it's not like in class where you just follow along in the book or something."

I laughed again and didn't even try to hide it this time, since I was thinking of being in Greenwald's class and how he mumbled so bad you could barely hear him. Then he'd get all pissed if you asked a question and say you weren't listening.

"What an asshole," I blurted, but Dustin just ignored me and started reading from his paper what the guy told him.

"At first he said all this stuff about the plants and the trees and the waves that were there, and how everything was together somehow. And then he said how the universe goes on forever and that everything was a part of that, too. And then he kept saying how I'm not what I think ... I mean, that I'm not just the stuff I think about ... like before I ever learned anything at school, or from my parents or anything ... I mean, back when I was really little, I guess ... and like that's how we start off connected to everything."

Dustin looked over at me and then looked down across his notes like he missed something.

"Wait. Okay ... then he said that nobody ever believes him ... I mean, that everybody thinks they know everything already ... but that they don't, really ... and so I should be open, though." Dustin said.

I laughed again. "Open to what—Jack in the Crack?" I said, and I thought it was a total burn but Dustin just stayed serious.

"I don't know ... to everything, I guess. He said it was like a car or a motorcycle engine, or like how a radio works ... I mean, that nobody ever knew that stuff was there before, either—"

Dustin stopped all of a sudden, then folded up his paper and put it back in his pocket. "That was pretty much it," he said. I could tell he was lying, though.

But then he got all quiet after that, and I guess I did, too, since it just felt weird after everything he was saying. And the storm was getting worse and a bunch of dark clouds were coming in over the mountain so we decided to make a run for it.

Dustin took off first, and as I followed him out through the trees and down along all the flooded streets towards 44th, I remember thinking everything he told me was just stupid. I mean, it was like some story he came up with to try to sound cool or to just mess with me or something. And then I could barely see him through the rain as we were running back towards Camelback Road, but I didn't even care if I lost him at that point.

Because that's when I remembered what he was saying about the universe going on forever and it kind of scared the crap out of me, to be honest. Because that's what I was having all the bad dreams about before ... I mean, they weren't even dreams, really, since the worst part was just lying there at night, scared to death since I couldn't stop thinking about it. But all that happened way before me and Dustin ever met, and I knew I had never told him about it, either, so it was just weird when he brought it up like that. But that's when I started getting that same, sick feeling again.

So for the whole rest of the way home, and then even when I got in the front door and my mom started yelling, I just kept going over it in my head ... Because how was it even possible?

I mean, for the universe to keep going on forever like that, and —

"Look at you. You're soaking wet," my mom said. But I wasn't really listening. Because it had to end at some point ... the universe, I mean. But then even if it *did* end, it still didn't make any sense ... because what was beyond *that*, then? And —

"You're going to catch pneumonia," she added, but that's what she always told me. And even if it were true, I mean, even if there was really something beyond all that, then that would mean there was no end ... and how could there be no end? ... Because it had to end at some point.

Until later that night as I was lying awake in bed, and with the storm getting worse and the thunder crashing down around our house, I guess I kind of freaked out about the whole thing again. And I know it probably sounds like I was just being a baby about the whole thing, but I swear, *you* try and think about it for a while. It'll scare the living crap out of you. I remember waking my mom up a couple times that night, too, till she finally let me sleep with the light on.

I felt a lot better the next day, though, for some reason. The storm was gone, so it was back to being hot again, as usual, and I think I was just messing around in the side yard that morning or something. But I wasn't really that worried about it anymore, at least.

Then Dustin called and wanted to go back up to the same place, but on our bikes this time, and I knew he'd probably bring it all up again, so I just told him I was grounded, even though I wasn't really.

And then I guess I said some stuff to my mom about him, about how stupid he was acting lately, I thought, and how he always got everything he wanted all the time, too, thinking she'd understand, maybe. But then she just ended up saying the same thing she always did—and about all my friends, really—that "maybe you and (insert name) have been hanging around each other too much lately *anyway*." Only this time I sort of agreed with her.

So with the day to myself I decided to just go to my fort for a while. And I might as well tell you about that, too, since that's where I was hanging out a lot back then. It was just down the canal from our house in that dead orchard with all the weeds around—like right before you get to Camelback Road to your right there. I mean, everybody knows about it now, but I'm just saying so in case you ever go there you can find it, maybe. But that was back when I was still trying to keep it a secret, and I might not even have found the place myself if I hadn't ate it on my bike that time.

You should have seen it, too. I was riding along the canal with no hands, which was pretty stupid, I guess, but I was trying to read one of those Bazooka gum comic fortunes, like,

> THINGS AT LOOK YOU WAY THE CHANGE TO GOT YOU'VE

or something like that, but that's when I lost control and went flying over the handlebars and slid face-first down into that ditch right next to the orchard. And I guess I was lucky I didn't fly right into the goddamned canal, like my dad said later. I did scratch my arms up pretty bad and I got the air knocked out of me, too, I think.

But as I was cleaning myself off and checking to see if my bike was alright (even though it was a total piece of crap anyway, so I didn't care what happened to it, really), I looked over and noticed some wood showing through the trees towards the middle of the orchard. It was pretty hard to get back there, too, but I pushed my bike ahead of me and was able to clear a path through all the weeds until I got up close and could see there was an old fort somebody must have built in there. And it didn't even look that great at first, to be honest, and I still had to break through a bunch of branches and weeds that were covering the entrance, but once I got inside there it was pretty awesome.

I mean, it was like standing under this huge tree umbrella, with the trunk in the middle and the branches coming down all around from above. I could even fit my bike in there the place was so big. There were a couple sheets of plywood on the ground, so it was kind of like having a floor, in a way, and some smaller sheets were set up around the sides to keep all the weeds back, I guess. The weeds were really thick coming up over the boards, too, and the way they met up with all the branches coming down — there was no way anybody could see you in there. There was some garbage left behind from whoever was there before, but it was mostly just some rusted beer cans and cardboard and stuff so it wasn't that bad, really. There was even an old plastic paint bucket you could sit on if you wanted.

Anyway, it was the greatest place I had ever found, so I was afraid if I told anybody they might ruin it. I mean, I had planned on telling Dustin, I guess, but that was around the same time he started acting weird so I hadn't even told him yet.

But like I was saying, that was that day right after he first brought up all the dream crap, and I remember lying to him about being grounded because I felt bad about it ever since. There was a lot going on, though, so it wasn't just the stuff about Dustin. And my mom had said I had to keep checking in from then on, too, so I actually was kind of grounded in a way. I still had enough time to go to my fort, though.

So I grabbed a couple Pop-Tarts, borrowed my dad's transistor radio, and managed to sneak a few smokes from my stash in the side yard before I left. I always just hid a few in my sock so I wouldn't get busted with a whole pack. But as I headed out of the driveway, I noticed my front tire was low so I had to go up to the gas station to fill it up first.

But that's when I started worrying that Dustin was going to see me, or that someone else might see me and that it might get back to him, somehow. So when I got to the alley, I stopped to eat a Pop-Tart and came up with some story to tell him just in case. And I can't even remember what it was, exactly ... something like ... *my mom said I was still grounded for being out in the rain for so long ... but that it was okay if I went up to the gas station to fill up my tire real quick, but only if I came back right away ... but that I couldn't go out in the rain ever again,* or something like that.

And I knew it sounded stupid, and that he wouldn't believe me anyway, but I went over it a couple times before I got up there, thinking I was going to see him, probably. Nobody was around, though, so once I fixed my tire, I got a Freezie at Circle and then headed back towards the fort through the alley again, since I was still trying to stay hidden.

It was pretty awesome back there, too, though, by the way, since the back alley was just for garbage trucks to pick up garbage, really, so nobody ever went back there but us. And you never had to worry about the trucks coming through either, since they came by so early and only once a week, I think. But it was this perfect dirt street that ran behind all the houses, with weeds and broken stuff everywhere, and a bunch of garbage cans you could kick out on if you wanted.

It was way better on a motocross bike, though, and all I had was that little piece-of-crap, orange ten-speed back then, which was probably why my tire was leaking in the first place since there were stickers everywhere and it couldn't handle it. I still went through there all the time, though, and even on a piece-of-crap bike like I had you could do a banzai run if you wanted. Just flying down the gravel pathways, switching back and forth between the high, dry grass, dodging all the garbage cans and whatever else might have been there, and you just try to get through as fast as you could.

I didn't feel like doing a banzai that day, though. I was just trying to stay on the gravel so my tire would last, and something was bothering me ever since I left the corner anyway. I mean, it was all the stuff my sister Llory was saying about becoming a compulsive liar and how certain people just start doing it without even knowing it.

"Because that's how it happens," she said. "You start off with your first lie, and even though you feel completely justified, it just leads to another one after that, and then you have to lie again to cover the last one, and then it just goes on from there until your whole life becomes a lie and you end up living in a complete nightmare."

I mean, that's kind of what she said, at least, so I was worried I was becoming a compulsive liar ever since. And I had just made up that whole story to tell Dustin, along with saying I was grounded when I wasn't in the first place.

My sister was older than me, though, so she was always saying stuff like that, trying to scare me into doing the right thing, I guess. So I figured there was a chance she just made up the whole compulsive liar thing to try and stop me from lying so much. But then she'd be lying, too, is what I started to think, until I remembered when she told me how *white lies* were okay, though, since they were the kind of lies that never hurt people, or something like that. But that's all I was doing then, is telling white lies, really.

But it wasn't just the stuff about Dustin, like I said, so when I got to my fort I started thinking about everything else for awhile.

Like about Pam Athena, who was this girl from Greece that sat ahead of me in one of my classes, and I guess I kind of liked her but I was never sure if she liked me, since she always had this disgusted look on her face for some reason ... And then that fat-ass Eddy Ludd had been bothering me again, and he was actually one of my best friends before that, but then he was just being an asshole to me all the time, and there was nothing I could do about it, either. And, no, I never called him a fat-ass to his face, but I kind of wish I would have, now that I think of it .... And then my dad had been yelling at my brother all week, saying he had to get the hell out again for some reason, but that meant I was never going to see him again, probably, even though he told me he'd be around, but I still didn't believe him. Because my brother had been living on his own before that, till the guys he was living with burned down the house where they were living at, so my dad was just being a jerk about the whole thing, really. And my sister had moved out a few months before, so I never really got to see her at all anymore, even though she still came around with her friends once in a while, but I never knew when I was going to see her, though ... And then Greenwald was bothering me all the time, like I said, and then that stuff with Dustin, and he was acting weird even before all the dream crap happened...

But I was down in my fort, and I had a smoke lit already, and I had my dad's radio hanging from one of the branches from above, and I knew no one could see me in there either, so they wouldn't know where the music was coming from ... And then I started thinking about some other stuff all of a sudden, and I could imagine like I was one of those guys on TV or something.

And it was nice in the shade, and I had my paint bucket to sit on, and I was just sitting there smoking and thinking about different stuff, but I swear it was like I was one of those guys somehow ... so I just sat there and listened to the radio after that, and I smoked like I was one of Kelly's heroes, or James T. West or that guy in *High Plains Drifter*, or even the Fonz would have been cool, I guess ... but he didn't smoke, I don't think, or at least they never showed it on TV if he did ... but that last episode where he jumped that shark was just stupid ... And then I was back to being myself again, like my life was some weird movie, but I was the one that was starring in it or something ...

And the songs on the radio were playing along to everything I was thinking and the words they were singing were exactly how I was feeling (like that older version of myself loves that stupid old Dylan song now "It's Alright, Ma (I'm Only Bleeding)"). But back then it was "On And On" into "Night Moves" and "One Is the Loneliest Number" and "Baker Street" and "Year of the Cat" and "Hotel California" and "How Deep Is Your Love" and "Baby Come Back" and "Take It To The Limit" and "Fire And Rain" and "Yesterday" and "Philadelphia Freedom." And then "Blinded by the Light" again, and "Daniel" and "Rhiannon" and "Space Oddity" and "Sarah's Smile" and "Imaginary Lover" and "Doctor My Eyes" and "Evil Woman" and "I've Seen All Good People" and "Benny And The Jets" and "My Life," and even that song "Love Is Like Oxygen" was kind of cool ...

But I felt a lot better after I listened for a while. *And I felt like I could ask Pam Athena to dance and not be nervous or even care if she said no, and maybe my brother could stay at the house with us and that my parents would be nice to him from then on, and maybe my sister would even come back home ...*

And that Eddy Ludd would get off my ass, and that Greenwald would get in trouble somehow, and that Dustin would stop acting so weird, and that school would be easier ... and that my parents would love me still, and maybe I could be more like those guys on TV, the ones who didn't seem to care at all ...

And then a car was going by really loud up on Camelback Road, and it brought me back to listening to another song on the radio, and: *"Are you reelin' in the years ..."* the guy was singing, and I swear he said something about *"have you had enough of lying"* at the end. So I lit another smoke and got up for a while, and then I started thinking about the actual sound of the music that was coming through the radio ... and it reminded me of what Dustin was saying, or what that guy had told him in his dream, I guess ... and I noticed how the antenna was pointed towards the sky, and I had never really thought about it before, about how it all worked, I mean. And then I guess I felt a little sick again, to be honest, kind of like I did the night before when I freaked out about everything ... and I knew I should probably get back anyway, but I was still thinking about some other stuff, though ...

Like that sound I never heard before, and that beautiful orange light, and how I followed it down the hall, and how I found the dining room table on fire where my mom had left a candle burning, and the flames were almost to the ceiling, so I ran into my parents' room, and in my mind I was screaming, but I knew they couldn't hear me because I couldn't even say the words to tell them what was wrong, so I shook my dad really hard, and then everybody was yelling because I still couldn't say a word, but I led them to the fire, and my dad pulled in the hose from outside and stopped it all, somehow. But I was the hero my mom said, even though I couldn't say a word ... and if I could only do that every night ... to be the hero, I mean ... but then the house would get burnt down, eventually. And then that dream I had later ... where I was floating on a raft out in the middle of the ocean, but I knew it was just this idea I had of what the ocean was like since I'd never really even been to the ocean before ... but it looked like it went on forever, too ... I mean, even though I knew it didn't from what I learned about it in school ...

But what was I saying again anyway? Oh yeah, my tire ended up going flat so I had to walk my bike all the way home.

What the scientist actually said in Dustin's dream:

"We are a part of these waves as well as everything around us. However, there are certain things I wish to tell you with regard to my experience, for the research I had attempted was held back by the close-mindedness of the scientific community as a whole. From their reluctance to acknowledge the hidden fields of information that serve to balance all other previously discovered laws. That besides the more obvious formations of energy, there is an unseen web of living creativity interwoven throughout our singular universe, one that lies behind the organization and evolution of all prior known existence ...

And although I was unable to accumulate enough data for a proven theory (mainly due to the current limits of our perception), there was always an underlying sense from within myself of a connection being made on a level far beyond our scientific ability to articulate. Nonetheless, I could literally sense these connections being made all around us, and concluded that through our subconscious and intuitive faculties, we must unknowingly serve as a conduit ...

Although, to continue to express these ideas publicly only contributed to the hardships of my family, therefore I continued my research in secret, albeit, unsuccessfully, till my body's end. However,

I have come here now to express my conviction through an avenue by which confirms my very theory ...

And might I add upon reflection, as to the current position of human existence, that there is no rationality for our present state of scientific and spiritual arrogance. Since as far as we have come, there is still so much more that exists here among us and throughout our singular universe that we are still unaware of, as well as other realms that will forever remain beyond our human perception—and for good reason ...

However, there are certain realities we must eventually become aware of if we are to spiritually and scientifically evolve as a species. Until then, however, we should keep our minds open and remain modest to the complexities of our current levels of perception ...

For I am aware that there has always been human reluctance with regard to the advancement of science and technological innovation, which is understandable, and in many ways has worked to our advantage in helping to moderate the possible negative outcomes of such premature growth. However, this same natural skepticism has also been exploited by those who historically consider these changes as a threat to the existing religious and political social order. Unfortunately, however, now it is the academic and scientific communities themselves who have again become entrenched in their initial discoveries and related dogmas, just as they did when I existed. For it is the most arrogant among us who still threaten the imagination, with the hope of protecting their own prior published works ...

Although true creative human innovation was never meant to be used as a pedestal for the human ego, or as a means to an end for financial or political gain, but most importantly, as a vehicle for the expansion and evolution of the human spirit. For these are not our ideas and never have been, but only the various forms of information awaiting our discovery and utilization, and should only be seen as a gift in return for the openness and courage necessary to be a vehicle for such growth ...

For it has already been well documented that some of our most significant "creative discoveries" have come to us serendipitously or just by being open to a particular direction of research, having very little or nothing to do with any specific human ability or forethought. So it is clear to me now, that at this stage of human development, that meaningful scientific, spiritual, and societal advancement can only move forward through the reopening of our minds and the redirection of our thoughts and solidified beliefs. We should remember the faith upon which all scientific discoveries and societal advancements were first developed. We should revisit the source of our own being from which all spiritual growth has evolved.

We should understand that to look beyond an already established certainty is to embrace the possibility of a new and undiscovered truth, so that finally, we can be open to the idea that these alternative fields of informational intelligence actually exist ...

For this is nothing new, and can already be related to our intuitive and spiritual connections being made with these realms, regardless of our current reluctance to it. For that which is most unexpected will later be most obvious, just as the invisible transmission of radio waves along with the entire electromagnetic spectrum were considered inconceivable just a short time ago. Or that the existence of other galaxies were undetectable before the advancement of high-powered telescopes. And even now, the newest discoveries in the various microscopic realms, as well as our recent acknowledgement of the countless meta- and multi-verses that exist beyond our singular universe, ones that encompass a completely different set of physical and spiritual laws, still farther beyond our perception.

So we must remind ourselves that these realms, both quanta to the infinite, were with us all along, regardless of our inability to first detect them, just as these currently undetected realms surely exist before our imagination has had a chance to conceive of them. However, besides our openness of mind and scientific faith, it is usually (as with the examples just given) our inspired imagination that serves as a catalyst to move beyond our limited perception, the same miniscule, human perception we now insist is at its limits ...

Although, it struck me as I existed, that with regard to these unacknowledged fields of information, that no additional instruments will be needed to eventually perceive them. Meaning, since our intuitive and subconscious sensibilities have been evolving for hundreds of millions of years, and will continue to evolve, so that humanity itself will be the eventual vehicle through which these transmissions will later be defined and utilized. Therefore, human perception can eventually outgrow the limits of its own scientific instrumentation or "methods." So to focus our intelligence and intuition through human cooperation over long periods of time is how to magnify our perception beyond our current limits, for we are the very instrument we seek ...

I had only hoped to expedite this process in my human lifetime, to possibly help expand our limited perceptions a bit further, since the little we have discovered so far should encourage only humility,

not hubris ... I only wish you could see these things from my new perspective, out here in the great perfection ..."

Singularity

What we don't know
Is that time can stand still
And that restless men wait patiently
As the violence unfolds
And good people mean well
And the choice is in our memory

And the blood will flow back in our veins
We'll redesign life's destiny
As people first refuse to change
It's just the fools and their machines
Making radio waves

And what we don't know
Is that luck first started
When a gambling man refused to play
And the smartest thief said
If you want more money
Then the greatest scam is honesty

And the blood will flow back in our veins
We'll redesign life's destiny
As people first refuse to change
It's just the fools and their machines
Making radio waves

And what we don't know
Is the universe ends
In a galaxy six feet away
And through all the ages
Till the great perfection
It's in every mistake we've ever made

II

I was already hanging out with Dustin again a few days later, so it wasn't like we ever stopped being friends, really. And he never even asked me why I wasn't still grounded, so he probably knew I was lying the whole time, anyway. He was just like that, though. I mean, he never wanted to embarrass anybody or hurt anybody's feelings — unlike a lot of people. Anyway, he never brought up the stupid space crap again, which was good since I was still feeling weird about it. But a couple weeks after that, on that Monday before school, he started telling me a bunch of other stuff.

I remember walking up the street to catch the bus that morning, too, dodging all the cracks along the sidewalk so I wouldn't hurt my mom at all. And I knew it probably wasn't going to hurt her anyway, but still. And then I was thinking of how screwed up everything was, since my brother had finally gotten kicked out that weekend, or as my dad put it, "Your brother Michael moved out last night." But I could hear everything through the wall when it happened, and from the way everybody was yelling, I would have moved out, too, if I was him. I figured I was never going to see him again, though. Jerk never said goodbye, either.

And that whole weekend sucked, actually, since Dustin had gone up camping with his parents *again*, which pissed me off every time since my parents never did anything like that. So I just sat around bored and went to my fort a couple of times, and then I guess I watched *Poseidon Adventure* again that Sunday night. But then that stupid theme song was stuck in my head the next day, which made everything seem even worse. "There's got to be a morning ..." *Oh god*.

The bus stop was just up the street on that corner where the road splits out towards 44th, and there was a big tree in that yard there that you could stand under if you wanted. But when I got there, Dustin wasn't there yet so I waited on the curb with a couple kids from the neighborhood I didn't like very much. It was that brown-haired girl with all the books who never said anything, and that spaz Ron Cadwell who really bothered me, to be honest.

"*Heeeey*, ol' McDonald!" Cadwell said, trying to imitate the Fonz, I think, but he sounded more like Ernest Borgnine or somebody. "How about those McDonald's hamburgers?" he added, "Two all-beef patties, special sauce, lettuce, *cheeeeese* — you get a deal, right?"

I couldn't think of anything to say, so I just gave him a mean look.

"Just kiddin'," he said, "Just kiddin', *man*. Keep on truckin', disco sucks, *man*!" He had that stupid smile that covered his whole face, too.

The girl with all the books looked at both of us funny, and Cadwell switched his attention when some other kids showed up, thank god. Then Dustin got there right as the bus was coming around the corner, and once we shook hands and got in line, I could tell something was bothering him.

"Remember what I told you before?" he asked.

"Not really," I said, already worried he was going to bring up something weird.

"The special sauce, *man*!" Cadwell joked, from behind us.

"Shut up, *Cadwell*," I muttered.

"Just kiddin', just kiddin', *man*."

Dustin leaned towards me so nobody could hear him, but then the bus doors opened with that *Pssssss* sound and scared the crap out of me for a second.

"The same thing happened while I was up camping," he said under his breath. "I mean, I had another dream like the last one."

"Oh, cool ... How was it up there anyway?" I asked, trying to change the subject. I really didn't want to hear about his stupid trip, though, either.

Dustin gave me a strange look. "It was somebody else saying stuff, though," he said, "I'll tell you in a minute."

Then the line started moving and I was worried he was going to bring up the same crap again, so that's when I started to think I should just tell my parents this time or something. Or that maybe my sister would know what to do when I saw her again.

"Just don't tell anybody," Dustin said as I followed him onto the bus, and I swear it was like he could hear what I was thinking right then. Because I had already told my brother about the last dream, even though I was pretty sure he didn't believe me, and it was just the stuff about the universe, really, since that's what freaked me out so much. And I was probably never going to see him again anyway — my brother, I mean.

But then I was walking through the aisle behind Dustin, thinking all this stuff, and he turns around and gives me this weird look again all of a sudden, like he really could hear what I was thinking somehow.

"WELL DON'T TELL ME ABOUT YOUR STUPID DREAMS, THEN!" I yelled as loud as I could from behind him, but I was yelling it in my mind just to test him, I guess. And he didn't turn around or say anything after that, so I figured the whole thing might have just been a coincidence. I mean, it was pretty weird, though, and he might have just pretended not to hear me, to throw me off maybe.

Anyway, we took our usual seats in the middle section, not far from Cadwell and the girl with all the books, which is pretty much where we always sat—halfway between the rich kids up front and the assholes in the back.

And I know I never called them assholes back then, since they were the guys I thought were so cool, actually. And if *they* thought you were cool, then everybody thought you were cool for some reason, which is why everybody wanted to be friends with them, I guess. But that was the weird part, since they were just assholes to people most of the time.

I ended up hanging out with them later on, though, so I was kind of being an asshole, too, for a while there. But this was way before all that, back when I still wasn't cool enough, I guess, even though I was already friends with most of those guys from before we even started middle school.

But I'm getting way off track with all the asshole stuff here, since I wanted to tell you what happened with Dustin first, like I said. And he didn't even care about those guys anyway. I mean, it was probably because he had just moved there the year before, so he didn't know who they were at all. But he hardly said anything about them, really. They never bothered him either.

Once we were on the bus, Dustin sat near the window and got quiet all of a sudden. And then we started out towards 44th and that stupid *Poseidon Adventure* song was stuck in my head again.

"It was pretty fun," Dustin said, out of the blue, like he wanted to answer my question, finally.

"Cool," I said, but I still didn't care, to be honest.

And then he started telling me about how they were up near Flagstaff or somewhere around Mogollon Rim, I guess, and how they cooked marshmallows or something like that, and that's when I realized I'd much rather hear one of his stupid dream stories than about another boring camping trip.

"So what happened, though," I interrupted, and he seemed glad I asked and started telling me everything.

"Okay, I was lying there in my tent Saturday night," he said, "and it was kind of scary since I couldn't see at all ... and I could hear there was something out in the woods, too. So I kept shining my flashlight out through the trees whenever I heard anything until my dad said I had to stop. But then I must have fallen asleep, because the next thing I knew it was like I woke up alone out in the woods somewhere ... I mean, it was like I must have been sleepwalking or something—"

The bus stopped right then so Dustin hesitated as some regular kids got on and took a few of the empty seats in front of us. He seemed excited to tell me the rest, too, but he waited till the bus started moving again so no one could hear him, probably.

"So then I was out in the woods somewhere," he whispered, "and I wasn't feeling very good either ... And then I started to worry I was never going to find my way back again. It was almost light out, too, so I thought it was the next day already ... and then I thought my parents might have left, too. And everything just felt so real, like the last time I told you ... I kind of knew I was dreaming still, though—"

"*DICKWAD!*" Someone yelled out the window from the back of the bus, so we all looked outside to try to spot the dickwad, I guess, but it was just this guy riding a ten-speed alongside us down 44th. And you could tell right away it was Dan Ares who was yelling, just from the way he was trying to sound so cool. I mean, I know how to do it now, too, I guess, since you just let every word slope off at the end. But Ares was the main asshole back then for sure, with his awesome new motocross ultra-lite, and his perfect, feathered hair all the time, and he always had the coolest clothes, too. I hated those stupid painter's pants, though.

"WHAT A *DICKWAD!*" Ares yelled again, but this time he was yelling it from the seat right behind us, since the dickwad was flying right past us while we were stuck in traffic for some reason. And the guy didn't even look like a dickwad, really, so Ares went back to his seat since nobody was laughing at that point.

Dustin leaned forward like he was trying to concentrate and then went back to his story like nothing had even happened. "But then someone else was there," he said, "like the last time … I mean, all of a sudden this lady was there in the woods with me …"

Then Dustin got even more excited while he was talking about her, and as the bus turned up one of the roads towards the mountain and up this big hill that led up through the rich neighborhoods, his voice got even louder, right along with the engine.

"BUT THEN EVERYTHING JUST LOOKED REALLY WEIRD ALL AROUND ... LIKE THERE WEREN'T ANY COLORS ANYWHERE—BUT IT WASN'T EVEN BLACK AND WHITE EITHER. IT JUST LOOKED DIFFERENT SOMEHOW ... LIKE A REFLECTION ... LIKE THOSE MIRRORS WE SAW THAT TIME ... IN THAT PLACE, THAT PLACE AT LEGEND CITY ..."

Dustin could see I wasn't following. "*AT LEGEND CITY!*" he said again, but right then the engine died off at the top of the hill, so it was like he was yelling it for a second.

"*YEAH, AT LEGEND CITY!*" Cadwell mocked from across the aisle, but nobody paid attention.

"Just kiddin, just kiddin, *man*," Cadwell said, like he thought Dustin was mad at him.

"Like those mirrors we saw in there," Dustin explained from under his breath, "In that place we went to ... *at Legend City*."

Legend City was this amusement park we used to go to, but I still didn't know what he was talking about, really. "Okay, *Legend City*—what about it?" I asked, just to get him off the subject.

"The Laugh Tunnel!" Dustin remembered, "*No, wait* ... Tunnel of Laughs! I mean, that's what it was like in the dream everywhere, with all those mirrors—remember?"

And I never remembered it being called the laugh cave, or whatever it was he said, but I knew the place he was talking about right when he said it, even though he must have forgotten I never went in there, actually. And it wasn't because I was afraid either. I just thought the place looked stupid with all the yellow ropes and stuff hanging out front, like it was just for little kids, probably.

"Yeah, right ... okay, that *was cool*, I remember," I said, and I felt bad for lying, but it was easier than trying to explain everything again. I was getting kind of pissed he brought it up, though.

"But that's what it looked like," Dustin said, "like when you look in those mirrors like that, how it goes on and on forever."

"Cool," I said, but it just reminded me of the same crap about the universe again, so I was glad I never went in there, to be honest.

And then the bus started picking up the rich kids, who were always the last to get picked up on the way to school, by the way, so you could tell they were getting special treatment. And the same thing happened on the way home, too, but just the opposite, since the driver went right past all our stops and straight up the mountain to drop them off first. And I even asked the guy once if he could just drop us off along the way since we were going right past all our houses anyway, but he said he'd get in trouble if he did. But what an asshole, though, I thought, and whoever was telling him to do it, too.

Anyway, Dustin kept telling me his story, and then more and more kids were talking so nobody was really paying attention anymore. And to be honest, I kind of lost track for a while, since I was still thinking about the rich kids, I guess. Because that's when we made our last stop at the top of the hill along this big mountain ridge where this one super rich kid always got on. He sat right behind the driver, too. What an a—

"So then we were walking through the forest," Dustin said, "and I thought she was showing me the way back to our camp, maybe. But I didn't care at all, since everything looked so awesome there … I kept looking up through the trees, and the stars were everywhere, even though it was already light out, kind of … but it looked like a reflection up there, too. Then we came out of the forest and walked out into this big field, and there were all these pools of water everywhere … and then the trail we were on split off into all these different directions………………..……………….

like a maze on top of the water……………
………………………… she made the trail open up ahead of us………………......like she had these powers………………....…another big field after that…………….…………………………………………
……………………………………………………
……….………………....……….these huge trees were there again…………………………………..
…………………………..………………… looked like buildings……………... branches with windows………………………………………………
……………………….
……………………………………………………………………
…………………………..

Dustin nudged me.

"You even listening?" he asked.

"*Yeah*," I blurted, "Trees with windows. It sounds *cool*, though." I said. But I had spaced out through most of what he was telling me, since I was thinking about a bunch of other stuff at that point. I mean, mostly the stuff about my brother again, and why nobody ever said anything about the rich kids, and then about the universe, I guess, and why I never went in the stupid laugh cave, or whatever it was he called it. I mean, I should have just gone in there, probably … And then about Pam Athena …

"But then we were just standing there, looking back at everything," Dustin said, "and it was like I felt better somehow, too. And then she just started telling me stuff ... like the last time. It was just different this time, though ..."

Right then the bus pulled into the school parking lot and I could tell Dustin was finished with his story at that point. But then I was kind of pissed, actually, since I wanted to hear the end at least.

"I'll just tell you the rest later," he said, and as everybody got up to leave, the assholes were barging up the aisle already, with Ares leading the way, of course.

"What's your problem, *McDonald*?" Ares said, since I guess I was looking at him weird.

"*Nothin'*, man. *That was* funny, though, when you yelled at that guy," I said, but it sounded all awkward when I said it, and Ares just walked right past me anyway. And Radick was right behind him, giving me that smartass look, as usual, since he was one of those old friends of mine from grade school, so he was pretending not to know me, I guess. But I think he was just embarrassed about all the stuff that happened with Pat before, and I should probably tell you about that later, too. And Dustin was just staring out the window when I said that stuff to Ares, so

I don't think he even heard me. I felt pretty stupid when I said it, though.

And Dustin never did tell me the rest of his story that day, since I guess he ended up going home sick for some reason. I mean, he said he was sick anyway. Everybody knew you could trick the nurse pretty easy, though; thermometer under the armpit, or I used to just say I wasn't feeling good so I could get out of class for a couple hours. I just figured he was faking it at that point, though.

But then he was out for the next couple of days so I didn't know what to think, really. I called him a few times but there was never any answer, and I even went by his house after school the next day, but there was nobody there either.

So it was weird when I saw him the day after that, just standing in this dirt lot up along Camelback Road for some reason. He didn't even look sick, either. I just happened to be riding past there, too, so I didn't expect to see him at all. But there he was, just standing out there, staring at the construction they were doing or something.

I almost flipped my bike right in front of him when I rode up, too, since my front brake was all messed up. I mean, my brother had helped me fix the leak in my tire, but now the brake wasn't working right, probably from when I wiped it on the canal before. I almost ate it pretty bad, though, and there were cars flying by everywhere so the whole thing kind of stressed me out, to be honest.

I hated that stupid bike, too, by the way. It was this bright orange, mini-style ten-speed that was way too small for me, and Ares and all those guys were always calling it the "dork bike," which is what I ended up calling it, too, since I hated it so bad. And all I could think of whenever I was riding the stupid thing was the awesome red motocross bike I had gotten for my twelfth birthday. The same one I only got to ride for like two hours before some assholes stole it up at Tower Plaza Mall that same day. And I swear I only left it unlocked for like thirty seconds before I ran back outside, but it was too late. So then my parents got me the dork bike—I mean, I guess with the idea that nobody would ever want to steal it. And they were right, too, since I left that thing lying around unlocked pretty much everywhere I went for like two years and nobody would even come near it.

Anyway, I was thinking all this stuff while I was trying to fix my brake when Dustin came over and met me near the road.

"Hey, man," he said, and he acted kind of guilty as he grabbed the brake cable out of the way to try and help.

"I got it," I said.

And I asked him what he was doing there, and I barely remember what he told me right then; something like he was just messing around, but I could tell he was lying for the most part. Like how he was feeling a lot better since he had just had a cold for a couple days, but, like I said, he didn't look sick at all. And then he started in with all these questions about what he had missed at school, and he was saying a bunch of other stuff to try to make it sound like he wasn't lying, so I just interrupted him.

"Weren't you going to tell me what that lady said?" I asked, right as my wheel started moving. "From your dream, remember?"

Dustin gave me this weird look, and I figured the dream thing would throw him off since he was probably lying about all that, too.

"Okay ... I didn't know if you heard me," he said, and then headed up the sidewalk all of a sudden.

"I heard you," I said, and right then my brake started working, and I figured I burned him pretty good at that point.

"LET'S GO TO MY HOUSE THEN ... SOKIN, REJA, NARGA, DA NOFOOK—" Dustin yelled, but I couldn't make out the last part since a big truck went by really loud. I just figured he needed to go to the bathroom or something.

"Okay ... WAIT UP!" I yelled, but as soon as I pushed off I could tell there was something wrong with my bike still, so I circled back around in the lot a few times till my wheel started moving again, finally.

When I caught up with Dustin he had crossed the street already and was heading up Camelback Road along the sidewalk towards his house. I tried to get him to jump on the handlebars so we could get there faster but he wouldn't do it, so I just walked alongside him with the dork bike.

His neighborhood was pretty close anyway, and it reminded me of all the rich kids for a second, too. I mean, his parents weren't totally rich, but they lived in these big, white condominiums with a gate out front, even though nobody ever stopped you. But Dustin always got a bunch of cool stuff from his parents, so I knew they were doing better than we were at least. He never acted like it, though. I mean, he never acted like he thought he was better or anything.

When we got to his house he said I could put my bike in the carport, but I could tell he was just being nice, so I left it laying out in the street hoping somebody might run over it, maybe.

And that was that day I got kind of pissed, though, actually, since right as we were walking up the driveway I could see his new YZ-80 dirt bike leaning up against the wall behind the cars there. And that's what I was talking about before, too, about how Dustin always got a bunch of cool stuff all the time, since a YZ-80 was the greatest thing you could ever get back then, and his parents had already gotten him one.

I mean, I had already seen it anyway, so I shouldn't have let it bother me so much, and he even let me ride it through the alley a couple of times, even though I messed up the gears a little that last time, I guess. But something about how nice it was went right up against all the trouble I was having with the dork bike and it just pissed me off, like I said.

"You been out riding at all?" I asked, trying to stay calm as we were standing there looking at it.

"Not really."

"Oh yeah ... you were *sick*," I said, and I guess he could tell I didn't believe him, because that's when he told me to get my bike out of the street since his dad would get mad if it was laying there. But then he made me park it right next to his YZ-80, so it was kind of like he did it on purpose, I thought.

Then he started yelling for his mom through the side door, so I forgot about my bike after that. And I guess we had to wait for her to answer before we could go in or something.

And I know it sounds stupid, but all I kept thinking at that point was that his mom was probably in there naked for some reason. But then she never answered, so Dustin went inside, and as I followed through the side door, I could hear a bunch of metal hitting up against something in the background, but I guess it was just some clothes his mom had in the dryer, Dustin said. And that's what I was saying, and it did kind of make sense, that his mom was probably in there naked since her clothes were in the dryer or something. But it wasn't like I was thinking about his mom or anything.

Anyway, then Dustin told me to wait for him in his room upstairs, since he was still trying to find her, I guess. And that's when I started getting kind of pissed again, actually, thinking about all the rest of the cool stuff he had up there.

And sure enough, right as I walked in, all his GI Joes were still standing there on his dresser, staring at me. He even had a couple new ones, too, I think, along with that red-haired, kung-fu-grip guy I could never talk my dad into getting me. And right next to that, leaning against the wall near his desk, was that blue light saber he got right after *Star Wars* came out. I mean, I ended up getting one, too, since they were pretty cheap, I guess, but mine was the cheapest kind so it was broke already. But Dustin had one of the good ones, so it was still in perfect shape with the batteries working and everything, so I took a few swipes around the room with the blue light just to check it out for a second. I almost stepped on one of his models, though—he had a bunch of cars and ships and planes spread out on newspapers on the floor all around. And there were Spitfires and Flying Tigers, and Gull Wing Corsairs hanging from the ceiling over his closet, along with a bunch of other planes I forgot the names of that were flying up there, too. And then he had all these cool posters up on the walls everywhere, and that awesome *Star Wars* one that nobody else had was hanging over his bed, I remember. It was kind of stupid, though, I thought, just how much stuff he had, really.

I mean, he even had his own pet bird in this big metal cage over near the window. We were always laughing about that, though, since it was this big old parrot named Pecker that his grandma had given to him. And I guess she named him Pecker since he was pecking at his cage so much when they first got him. But she had him for so long, and people started saying that word in a different way, I guess, but I don't think she ever heard about it, really. So when Dustin finally got him, they just kept calling him Pecker, I mean, out of respect for his grandma, probably. His parents were always trying to act like it didn't mean anything, though, and that was the best part, since me and Dustin would always call out his name really loud, like we didn't know what it meant, either.

"PECKER!"

"PECKEEEER!"

"HEEERE, PECKER!"

Wait, it was that day at his house in the kitchen when his mom was there, and his dad and his brother were around, too, but I think I just asked how Pecker was—and I didn't even mean anything by it, either, but then Dustin just started laughing and calling out for him really loud.

"PECKEEEEER!"

"YOU UP THERE, PECKER?"

"HEEEERE, PECKER!"

That's how it started anyway, so we were laughing about it all the time, even though his mom always got mad because she knew what we were doing, probably. And Pecker never said anything back, either, by the way. I mean, parrots are supposed to say stuff when you call them like that, but this one never did, for some reason. He always gave me this mean look, though, like he knew we were making fun of him.

"Pecker!"

Anyway, I thought it was funny. But then I was just standing there in Dustin's room waiting for him, looking around at all his stuff again. And I couldn't stop thinking about the kung-fu-grip guy, since I knew my parents would never get me anything like that. And that's when I just started feeling kind of sick to my stomach, in a way, and I didn't even want to be there anymore, to be honest. But then Dustin came in, finally, and I realized I still had the light saber in my hand, so I was kind of embarrassed about it.

"Pretty cool, *man* ... it still works," I said, but then I accidentally kicked one of his models as I was trying to put his saber back. He didn't notice, though. Then Dustin locked the door behind him and went over to the closet and grabbed some sort of school notebook from the shelf.

"I don't even think they believe me," he said, "and they keep saying it's normal having dreams like that."

Dustin went back and checked the door again, like his parents might be listening. "I never told them the whole thing, though ... You really want to hear it?" he asked.

And I guess I was still thinking about everything else at that point, and I kind of just wanted to go home, like I said, but I decided I might as well hear the rest. So I went and sat on this wood trunk over near the window. Pecker was right there, too.

"It was pretty weird, though," I blurted, "I mean, that first dream you told me was weird."

Dustin leaned against the dresser and was looking at his notebook like he changed his mind all of a sudden.

"It was still, *cool*, though ... I mean, I wish *I* had dreams like that," I admitted. *Along with all the other cool stuff you have and don't even seem to care about*, I thought. And I swear Pecker gave me a mean look right then.

Dustin pulled a yellow sheet of paper from his notebook and I remember it was all covered with stuff written in red ink.

"I don't even understand most of it," he shook his head, "but she was one of those storytellers ... or a fortune teller, I mean ..."

What the clairvoyant actually said in Dustin's dream:

"Spirit said I was a true artist once, though I have never considered myself in this way. Though who among us still has such a gift, free from the suffering of all the traditional mediums? As in the artist once removed by the stroke of a brush, or the creation of a melody ... or even the passage of a thought or intuition. To be held by the instrument of society's choosing.

However, with our ability there is no separation. For we are the direct liaison through which the infinite finds its human voice ...

Although the artist once removed must endure both the humility and distance in perspective necessary to develop their final works. We, however, are faced with the burden of directly hearing such a voice or, on the contrary, not hearing anything at all at times, which brings with it the even greater responsibility of being truthful about it rather than just creating more illusion ...

There are many of us, however, who have chosen this form of deception ... those who would rather forfeit their selfless role as translator as a way to be perceived as an actual source. These are the metaphysical plagiarists, the cosmic travelers, who in most cases create more suffering than was even necessary, the suffering of the yet to be realized, or the yet to be deserved ...

And although I had never taken part in these illusions, there is another path by which I am guilty, and that is to have altered the message I did receive with the selfish inclusion of my own judgment. And though I had actually meant well, it was through this subtle arrogance nonetheless, to believe I knew better than the message itself, which had created this distortion ... Because now it seems that the information I had once held back, which was the direct knowledge I believed would have hurt people, may very well have helped them ... Though this will never be known having never allowed for it ...

For these observations have been a part of our metaphysical truth from a very early age, that the gift to receive and comprehend these messages is to be taken with the greatest sense of honor and humility, which the artist once removed still values with integrity. For we all know intuitively that this clearer perception of energy was never meant to be used as a form of manipulation, or as a way to influence a future outcome as we see fit, but is only available for us to bring forward to the world as an honest reflection of it.

Although not to accept these limitations has been our downfall ... For I can see now that the arrogance we have cultivated with regard to our ability has corrupted our own expression of it, and has only contributed to the loss of humanity's trust. Therefore, I have come here now to express this awareness with the hope we can evolve back to our original, spiritual integrity ... Although, there are very few of us left who still possess this basic quality, to be more spirit than our preconceived societal identity ... to be an uncorrupted and selfless reflection of humanity ... and it isthroughghjkth—"

"DUSTIN!"

spiritualvisionsmysticrealizationsdivineencounters—

"GODDAMN IT DUSTIN, WAKE UP!" ... *totrulyreachaformakjhtvlevelwithinit* ... "WAAAKE UP!!" ... *theseinformsthatkllksjdhf ouriuwryspe—*

"But I couldn't hear the rest of what she was saying since my dad was yelling so loud."

"WAAAKE UUUUP, GODDAMN IT ... WAKE UUUPP!" Dustin imitated his dad like he was yelling out of his mind, but he did it in this really quiet voice, so it was pretty funny.

"And that's when I realized I was back in my tent, and my parents were there freaking out, I guess because they couldn't wake me up at first."

Dustin put the sheet of paper back in his notebook and then went over to the closet and stuffed it behind some clothes on one of the lower shelves. Then he changed his mind, I guess, and moved it somewhere in the back corner where I couldn't see it after that. And I don't even know what he was worried about, really, since the stuff he was telling me was so stupid I didn't even care about it.

Dustin laughed. "My dad was all mad, though," he said, as he went and checked the door again like he heard something. "He said I must have stolen his beer—like that's why I wasn't waking up."

"You did, though, right?" I asked, hoping he'd say he did since that would explain everything.

"Not really," he said, "I mean, I checked the coolers before I went to bed but there was none in there ... They're always hiding it now anyways, after the whole Pat thing."

And the whole Pat thing is what I was going to tell you about before, when me and Dustin were hanging out with Radick back then. And Dustin gave me this really sad look when he brought it up, too, like he still couldn't believe it.

I had already heard about his stupid dream, though, and now he was bringing up the whole Pat thing again, and to be honest, I was still feeling kind of sick to my stomach, so I just told him I had to go home after that. And I wasn't even worried about all the stuff he had anymore, or the story he just told me, since it sounded all made up anyway. I just remember feeling like everything was going wrong at that point, and I knew there was nothing I could do about it, either. Like when you're stuck in one of those classes you never wanted to be in the first place, but you're still getting forced into it.

The Clairvoyant

The mystery of all that's good
When every life's a part to play
I guess I misunderstood
I thought that I might be myself someday
Now that I can see through the veil
Now that I can see through
And now where all these houses stood
Are all these buildings lined like graves
To build a future half as good
And there are things I dare not say to you
Now that I can see through these walls
Now that I can see through

And the spirits told me when I was a child
To be open to the strange and the unknown
And to live my life with the grace of a child
For a reason with the faith of an angel
And if I am ever to lose my way interfering
With the lives of the future

To know that the truth
will be told either way
For a reason, in the form of an answer

The mystery of all that's good
When every life's a part to play
I guess I misunderstood
I thought that I might be myself some day
Now that I can see you

III

"Fugin' cops keep comin' 'round, tellin' me I gotta move an' shit, askin' me how I got here ... Like I did somethin' wrong to somebody, or like I gotta fugin' screw loose or some shit... Well, hell yeah, I got a fugin' screw loose, why the hell else would I be out here like this?"

My dad was the first one to tell us about Pat. It was on that Friday after school when me and Dustin and Radick were just hanging out at my house, not even doing anything, really, when my dad started in with all this stuff about how we should never go near him. We didn't even know about him.

"Just stay away from him," he said. "They're alcoholics. Probably diseased."

But as far as we were concerned, it was the greatest thing we ever heard; that there was a real-life bum hanging out down around Circle K. So we made up some excuse after that, like we needed to go to some friend's house or something, but then we headed straight up to the corner to try and see if we could find him. It did freak us out a little when we first saw him, though.

We were coming up the back way through the alley and headed through that narrow space between the liquor store and Circle K as a shortcut. But when we came through the other side, Pat was right there, all sprawled out on the ground and it scared the crap out of us since we didn't expect it.

"Got any change, fugers?" he asked.

"Shut up, you old geezer," Radick blurted.

"I'll kill you little fugers," he grumbled, and it looked like he was trying to come after us so we started running after that.

And Radick was always saying mean stuff, and he didn't even hang out with us usually, since he was always hanging out with Ares and those guys, mostly. I had known him ever since kindergarten, though, and he was pretty cool for the most part, and I was the one who introduced him to Dustin, and they got along all right.

"Why'd you say it, though?" I asked, as we made our way across the parking lot to the gas station.

"Because he *stinks*," Radick said, and started laughing like he was out of his mind or something. I mean, Radick always had this sort of high-pitched laugh anyway, but now he sounded like some kind of wild hyena or something. Me and Dustin were laughing when we heard it, too.

I was still pissed at him, though, since the guy was just asking for help, I thought, and I figured there was no way we were ever going to talk to him after that.

But then we ended up hanging out at the gas station for a while, just so we could watch him from a distance, I guess. And it was just weird seeing him there, really, since he didn't have any place to go, I don't think. And like how does it happen to people, I mean? But the longer we watched him, the more we could see he had it all worked out, actually. He just kept getting change from people, one after another, since they felt sorry for him, I guess. Then once he got just the right amount, he'd limp over to Circle K, buy a can of Pabst Blue Ribbon, go behind the buildings, and pound it as fast as he could, and then come back out to his spot near the shortcut and start taking change from people again. It was pretty awesome.

"Yeah, and these dump fugers got some money 'round here, you can tell ... It's like ther' feelin' guilty 'bout it, too ... like givin' me some change is gonna save 'em or some shit ... Well, that ain't gonna save ya, buddy,

but I'll take it anyway ... Now, what do these little fugers want again? I'll kill you little fugers!"

And I guess he could tell we were watching him at that point, since he was staring right back at us mumbling something, and we were just about to take off when I got one of the greatest ideas I ever had. And I swear it was like something just came over me, so I decided to go ask him.

"What are you doing?" Dustin yelled, but I was already halfway across the parking lot.

I almost changed my mind when I got up close to him though, since you could see all the dirt mashed into his hair and his beard, and there were stains of gross crap all over his clothes everywhere. And Radick was right, I guess, since he stunk pretty bad, too, and that yellow blanket he carried was all curled up around him with these stickers and crap all stuck in it. And then he spit a big ol' choge on the ground right in front of me and asked what I wanted, and I wasn't even sure if I still had the nerve to say anything at that point.

But somehow I just started explaining everything; about how we could never get anybody to buy us beer ever, and how those assholes tricked us that one time and got us a bunch of pop instead. And how we could get a bunch of money from our parents and that we'd split it all with him if he'd just buy us some beer, maybe. But he still wasn't saying anything, so I kept on explaining, and I can't even remember half the stuff I said to try and convince him when all of a sudden he smashed his fist against the ground really hard so I thought he was mad at first.

"*Hell yeah, I'll do it,*" he said, and then he spit another choge off to the side somewhere. Half of it was running down his chin, too.

"*M'name's Pat,*" he said, and then he reached out the grossest-looking hand I ever saw, since he wanted to shake on it, I guess.

"*Stay away from him. They're diseeeeased.*"
My dad's voice went off in my head. I still shook his hand, though.

Then Dustin and Radick came over, so I introduced them to Pat and I told them what the plan was. And I remember Radick let out an extra-wild hyena laugh so I knew he was happy. You could tell Pat was still pissed at him, though.

"*Gimee der money ... let's do it then!*" Pat said, as he started trying to get up.

But that's when we had to tell him we didn't have any right then. I mean, me and Dustin had a little change so we gave it to him, but we told him we'd be back later with enough to buy a whole case probably, Radick said.

So then Pat was just leaning against the wall counting the change we gave him and mumbling again, and Dustin had the idea that we should go get him some food and stuff, but when we asked him if he was hungry, he didn't seem to care, really. We still felt bad for him, though, so we all took off to go find some stuff at our houses and bring it back for him real quick.

When we got back, Pat was behind the liquor store all slumped over against the wall, trying to sleep, I guess. We had a bunch of stuff for him, though, so we woke him up anyway. Dustin brought a couple of baloney sandwiches and a thermos of milk he must have stolen from his dad or something. And all I could get was a half a can of Spam and some Bugles in a Ziploc bag, but only because my mom was around so I couldn't sneak anything else out. And Radick even brought some stuff but I can't remember what, exactly. Like some carrots, or half a banana or something. But then Pat just dug through it all real quick and he didn't even eat that much. He threw the baloney on the ground and only ate half a piece of bread, I think, and he was drinking some of the milk from the thermos but then he got all mad since we were watching him.

"*Go get chur' money, ya little fugers,*" he said, and then he started coughing real bad and dropped the thermos so the milk went everywhere. We all had to go eat dinner anyway, but our plan was to go get as much money as we could from our parents and meet back behind Circle in a couple hours, so we took off after that.

"Little dump fugers thinkin' ther' helpin' or some shit ... Like maybe I should come to ther' house an' meet ther' parents or some bullshit ... Hell, that's a good one. Me havin' dinner with one of those little rich fugers parents ... Like I need that fugin' bullshit ... Little dump fugers ... Another beer is all I need, or a bottle ... or a smoke, maybe ... Or maybe they wanna stop those fugers down on Van Buren from throwin' change out the window that's been heated up with a fugin' blowtorch ... Or stop those fugers that been tryin' to been lightin' me on fire an' shit ... Maybe they wanna help with that fugin' bullshit ... Little dump fugers ..."

Me and Dustin were the first ones to meet up back in the alley that night, and as we were walking towards the corner, I remember we were both pretty excited. I mean, just the idea that Pat was our friend made us feel a lot older, in a way, and then we were getting a bunch of beer, too, so we were pretty stoked about it.

But when we got to the corner, Pat was still lying in the same spot behind the liquor store, and Radick was there standing like ten feet away, since he was afraid to go near him, I guess.

"He won't move, I tried." Radick said, as he started pacing back and forth all upset. "I guess we're not gettin' anything now."

So me and Dustin went closer to check, but it was dark out already, and there was just this one orange light shining down from the top of the building, so we could barely see him all hunched over under his blanket there.

"Mr. Pat, it's us!" I joked, but he still didn't say anything and he wasn't moving at all, either. So that's when me and Dustin started thinking he might be dead or something. But then Radick got this idea and went and found this long stick from the alley and came back and started jabbing Pat in the neck with it.

"*Auuuhgg. Yug little fugers,*" Pat grumbled, and he got up pretty quick after that. But then he started blaming me for some reason, so I told him Radick was the one that did it. But at least it got him up, and he seemed okay, I guess, and we were just glad he still wanted to go ahead with our plan and everything.

So we talked it over and gave him all the money we had, which was about eight bucks altogether, I think, but instead of going to Circle like we told him, he kind of wandered out over towards the park for some reason. And I guess we thought he might take all our money at that point, but then he stumbled back the other way, and we realized he was just going around the corner to the liquor store drive-thru instead.

So we waited behind the buildings for him, and it seemed like it was taking forever, too. But when he came back around the corner, finally, he had a bottle of Beefeaters gin in one hand (which we never agreed on) and only two six packs of Pabst Blue Ribbon under his other arm instead of three six packs of Michelob like we told him.

"This is bullshit," Radick said, but Pat just handed us the beer and limped past us drinking his Beefeaters.

"I'mna need summa that Pabst later, too, ya little fugers," he said, and then he kind of laughed at Radick, it seemed like.

But we still had some beer, we figured, so we didn't worry about it too much. So we went over to the shortcut and with the orange light shining down, we all slammed our first beers as fast as we could, just like Pat always did. It was pretty awesome. We had it all counted out, too—that we all had four beers each, I mean—unless Pat got to it first, so we drank as fast as we could so we wouldn't have to give him any.

After we slammed a couple, though, we started slowing down, I guess, and we were getting pretty buzzed, I remember, but since we still had a six-pack left, we followed Pat over to one of his favorite drinking spots in the park behind the Jack in the Crack. And that's what he called it, too, so we were laughing the whole way. But when we got there, Pat said we had to hide along the fence in the dark since the cops would come around, probably.

It was still awesome, though, just sitting there along the fence drinking with Pat. And we could tell why he liked it there, too, since you could see all the cars and the lights and the people everywhere, but then nobody could really see us back there, either. And we were almost done with our third beer each, I think, and Pat was almost done with his Beefeaters. And we were still trying to hurry up, I guess, so we wouldn't have to give him any.

But that's when Pat started talking a lot, and it wasn't like he was just mumbling anymore, either. Because then he was telling us about the Vietnam War, since he was in it, I guess. And it sounded pretty scary, too. I mean, all the stuff he was saying, but I can't remember what, exactly. But the more he talked about it, the more pissed he got, and the more pissed he got, the more you could tell he still hated Radick—I mean, from all the stuff he did before, probably.

And then Radick started making all these smartass comments, as usual. Like, what did he *really* do in Vietnam, and why was he living out on the street and stuff, until Pat finally leaned over and grabbed Radick by the throat and started to choke him pretty good. And it was pretty funny at first, I thought, since Pat was always moving so slow, so it wasn't like he was going to hurt him at all, or, at least I didn't think. But then we could see Radick's eyes getting big, like I guess he couldn't breathe at all, probably, and his face looked funny bulging out like that, so I couldn't stop laughing, even though I felt kind of bad for him, really. But then Dustin offered his last beer to Pat, since he was out of his Beefeaters, I guess, so Pat let go of Radick like nothing had even happened. So it was Dustin who saved him, actually.

And then Radick was all mad, and I can't blame him, really. But we finished our last beers, and Pat was saying some funny stuff again, and I offered Radick a smoke, and he seemed okay after that.

The rest of that night I can barely remember, though, since we got pretty wasted. But let me just jump ahead and say that for the next three weekends in a row, my plan worked perfect and we partied with Pat like you wouldn't believe. And that's how we got to know him so good, too, since he told us a bunch more stories about Vietnam and about living on the street and everything, and even him and Radick got along pretty good after that first night.

But the cops had seen us hanging around him, I guess, and they kind of ruined everything when they pulled us aside that one day, even though everything they were saying sounded like bullshit, or like they were just trying to scare us, probably. And Pat wasn't even around when it happened, either, since he was gone during the week sometimes, so we couldn't even ask him about it. But I remember being out in front of Circle when they pulled up in their stupid squad car.

"*One-Adam-12, one-Adam-12,*" Radick mocked as they were getting out of their car to come talk to us. I used to love that show, too.

"Pat's bad news ... you guys know it, right?" the one cop said, and we were surprised they knew his name already.

"What do you mean, officer?" Radick asked, and they could tell he was being a smartass.

"You guys just need to stay away from him," the other mean-looking cop said, and he sounded just like my dad for a second.

Then Dustin asked why, and that's when they told us a bunch of stuff about Pat being sick from drinking so much, and how his leg was all infected and that it was still probably broken since he never went to the hospital to get it fixed right. And so that's why he was limping so bad, we figured.

"Gangrene's set in by now," the nice cop said.

"Gangrene ... *Jesus*," I said, and everybody stared at me. But I had heard about gangrene in a war movie I saw once. I mean, about all the leper colonies and all that, so it kind of freaked me out just thinking about it, to be honest. *He's diseeeeased.* My dad's voice went off in my head again, and I started to think he was right, probably.

"You guys should just stay away from him," the asshole cop said again, like he was making some final point about it. But as they were walking back to their car, we could hear they were still saying some stuff—something about Pat's days being numbered—like he was going to die soon or something. At least that's what it sounded like. We all heard them say it, too.

But Pat was our friend, so we weren't just going to *stay away from him*. And we still had a plan for him to buy us some more beer that coming weekend anyway. But everything the cops had told us kind of freaked us out, actually. I mean, the stuff about his days being numbered was the worst part, I guess. Because if Pat's days were numbered, then that meant all our days were numbered, really, and so then what the hell was the point to anything anyway? And then everything Pat was saying about how the cops and everybody were assholes, and how the whole world was all fucked up was probably true also, I mean.

So a few days later, me and Dustin went and found Pat lying in the shortcut since we figured we'd just ask him ourselves if it was true or not — at least the stuff about him having gangrene, anyway. He was sleeping when we got there, though, and we really didn't want to wake him, either, even though I was joking at first that I might poke him with a stick like Radick did. But Dustin could hear him snoring, I guess, so we knew he was alive still, and we just figured we'd see him again that coming weekend.

But when we came back around that next Friday, he was just gone, I remember. And it wasn't like during the week when he disappeared sometimes, since he always came back for the weekends since he knew we were getting beer and stuff. And Radick was saying the cops probably busted him, or they told him he had to leave again, and so maybe he did, finally. And Dustin thought they might have forced him to go to the hospital since his leg was so bad, I guess. But all I kept thinking was something bad must have happened, and I couldn't stop thinking it for some reason.

And sure enough, that very next day we found Pat's old blanket hanging over of one of the dumpsters behind the liquor store, so we knew he was dead after that, probably. I mean, there was just no way he'd leave his only blanket behind unless something really bad happened.

I remember walking around in a daze when we realized it, too. We just couldn't believe it, though. I mean, one minute you're friends with someone and partying and hanging out and everything, and then all of a sudden they're just gone after that.

We ended up over in the park later that day, but none of us really said anything. There was a wooden bench we used to hang out around, and

Dustin used a quarter to etch some stuff in it for him. *PAT WAS HERE – 1978.* He left the quarter sitting there next to it, too.

But that's when we decided we should probably try and quit drinking. At least for a while, anyway. I mean, we had only joked about it up until that point, like which one of us was going to end up like Pat first since we were always down there with him.

"Here's Radick a year from now," I'd say, and then imitate him limping around like he was out of his mind. *"You fugers! Give me some money ... I'm an old geezer now!"* I'd groan and then laugh like crazy. And Radick would say it was stupid what I did, but then he'd imitate me doing the same thing, like it was the greatest thing he ever came up with. But we were all making fun of Pat back then. I mean, even Dustin said some stuff, I think.

But after he was gone, we just felt bad for ever saying anything, and none of us wanted to end up like him, either. And Radick made a good point, I guess, even though it sounded kind of mean when he said it, but we didn't have anybody to buy beer for us after that anyway. But mostly out of respect for Pat, we all decided around the bench that day that that was it. I mean, from that day forward we were "on the wagon," which is what my mom always called it when my dad quit.

"Your father's on the wagon!" she'd say, and I used to picture him actually riding on a wagon when I was a kid. I mean, I knew what she meant after a while, and he'd always last a couple days, I guess, but then he'd take me on a drive as an excuse so he could sneak a beer or martini in a can and make me promise not to say anything. I mean, I still like going on drives with him.

Anyway, we were pretty serious about quitting at first, so we didn't even go down to the corner that much. And I think we were just riding our bikes around, or throwing rocks down at the canal and smoking cigarettes. But after being on the wagon for a couple weeks, I couldn't stop thinking about everything, and then I just felt like crap for the most part. We were so bored we could barely stand it, too.

So it was one of those weekends right after that, when my sister came to the house with her new boyfriend Dan Dioso, but I got up the nerve to ask him to buy us some beer, just like I did with Pat. And I wasn't even sure if he was going to do it or not, since my sister was saying a bunch of stuff to him before they left—something about us not being old enough, probably. But when I went back outside to meet up with Dustin after dinner that night, we found a twelve-pack hidden behind the bushes near the side yard, right where Dioso said he was going to leave it.

And then Radick showed up and let out this super loud hyena laugh so I thought my parents were going to hear us. But nobody came out, so we all slammed our first beers right there in the side yard next to my house before we even left that night. It was Michelob, too, this time. So then we headed up the street to the alley and ended up finishing the rest before we even got to the corner.

"Here's to Pat!" Dustin said, and we all made a toast in his honor.

And we remembered all the good times we had with him, and all the great parties. And we laughed about how slow he was and how he was always yelling at us for no reason. Or when he'd be telling us some story and then turn away and throw up all of a sudden, but then he'd just go back to what he was saying right after that like nothing had even happened. I mean, I know it sounds gross, but it was still pretty funny. And that first night when he was choking Radick was the funniest thing I ever saw, too, or, at least I thought so, anyway.

But then we got quiet since we knew we went back on our promise. I mean, we all felt guilty for not staying on the wagon like we said. And then

Radick was kneeling forward all hunched over with his beer hanging down, like he had gangrene all over his arm or something.

"*I don't give a shit, you little fugers!*" he grumbled, and he sounded just like Pat, so we all started laughing again.

And so then we were drunk and we finished our last beers and we smashed our last bottles against the wall in the alley. And then out behind Circle and the liquor store again, right where we found Pat's old blanket in the dumpster since he was dead.... But then Radick was saying some stuff, and it didn't feel right at all, like "*FUCK PAT ANYWAY!*" he was yelling ... And then I swear it was weird, since like something must have heard us, because right when we came around the corner, around the liquor store drive-thru, this guy came out of nowhere and this car almost hit him.

And there in the headlights, staring right at us and more wasted than we'd ever seen him before, was Pat.

"*Speak of the devil,*" he said.

And I swear I'm not lying since that's exactly what happened, and it scared the living crap out of us, too. And we actually did quit drinking for a while after that, since all of a sudden Pat was alive again, or like he came back to remind us we broke our promise since we were all laughing about it or something. But that's when Radick stopped coming around. I mean, he just hung out with Ares and those guys from then on, mostly.

I remember Dustin came on one of those drives with me and my dad around that time, and I was pretty embarrassed since my dad's hands were shaking as he was grabbing his beer at the drive-thru window. And Dustin was probably thinking the same thing I was, that Pat's hands were always shaking that way, too. He never said anything, though.

Idle Thought

I can't wait until now
So long ago decided this
It's deafening yet so loud
One but still divided

And if part of your soul knew
 the reason for this
And if I was just like you
And your spirit holds on to
 the things that you miss
Would you still tell me what I should do
We're forever alone to forever resist
And the strangest things are true

And some things you just know

A lonely audience
Waiting for this film to end
And through this awkward silence
The meaning's surely spoken

And if part of your soul knew
 the reason for this
And if I was just like you
And your spirit holds on to
 the things that you miss
Would you still tell me what I should do
We're forever alone to forever resist
And the strangest things are true
And some things you just know

IV

So, what was I saying again, anyway? I mean, there was another dream Dustin told me about, but some other stuff happened right before that, though.

Like on that last Friday before summer break started. I remember sitting in Ms. Pitt's class, waiting for the last bell to ring, thinking of how stupid it was that we had to come back on Monday and then again for another half day before they finally let us go. And I was just about to ask Ms. Pitts about it, too, when the bell went off into a thousand voices, chairs sliding, desks scraping across linoleum floors, people yelling outside at random, and then down the hall where I couldn't stop thinking if I was walking strange or not, and then past another girl I liked, but still too nervous, but then I was sure I was walking like an idiot, and then a stop at my locker and outside to the bus where Dustin had a spot saved for me in the middle section, as usual.

"*McDonald's a clown,*" someone yelled from the asshole section right as I got to my seat, but they were yelling at everybody pretty much.

"Yeah, it's Ronald McDonald," Cadwell joined in from across the aisle. *"Just kiddin' … just kiddin', man,"* he said, since he knew I was looking at him. *"Two all-beef patties … I mean, disco sucks, man …"*

I didn't even say anything, though. I knew it was Radick that started it, since now he was hanging out with Ares and those guys again, acting like we were never friends before.

And then Dustin was all quiet, just sitting there staring out the window for some reason.

"Just two more days," I said, as I got settled in, just trying to get him to say something, at least. "Well, half a day on Tuesday, but still," I added.

Then the bus started moving, and as we were headed out of the parking lot, even the assholes were quiet all of a sudden. And I guess everybody was thinking about the summer coming up, but it still just felt weird since Dustin hadn't said anything.

"I found this cool fort!" I blurted, but I was pissed at myself right afterwards, since I swore I wasn't going to tell anyone. And Dustin didn't even seem to care, really, and I was hoping he didn't hear me at first, but then he said something back, and I wasn't even sure if I heard him right.

"Yeah … He's moving anyway," Cadwell piped in, and I think I yelled at him after that.

Because that's when Dustin told me he was moving to a place up in north Phoenix called Moon Valley, so he was changing schools that next year and leaving right when summer break started.

Moon Valley. Jesus, I thought. I had never heard of the place, but the name sounded pretty stupid, though.

"So you won't even be around for the summer?" I asked, and I knew he just told me, but I was trying to be sure, I guess.

Because the same thing happened just a few years before, I remember, when my last best friend Clay Rupenthaul moved away. And I didn't even want to be friends with anybody after that, since every time you get to know somebody they just end up moving, usually. Rupenthaul moved to a totally different state, though. I mean, to like Texas or somewhere, so if Dustin was still in Phoenix, then—

"Maybe we can hang out still!" I said, trying to sound optimistic. We both knew it was over, though, since when your parents decide to move, there's nothing you can do about it.

When we got off the bus, I took Dustin to go see the new fort anyway. I mean, he promised not to tell anyone, and in a way I was hoping it might convince him to stay, I guess. But as we were walking through the neighborhood and down the side alley towards the canal, you could tell everything just felt different. And we weren't even talking at all, but I swear we were still saying a bunch of stuff. I mean, about the future, probably. Like when you know something's going to happen, but there's nothing you can do about it, so the whole thing's pretty stupid.

And then we were just skimming rocks along the canal and we weren't even saying anything still. And I guess it was just weird since we knew he was moving.

When we got to the fort, we lit up a couple smokes I had stashed and just hung out for a while. I let Dustin have the bucket to sit on and I found a good spot on the plywood near the entrance right across from him. I had fixed the place up pretty good since that first day, too, so I was proud to finally show it to someone.

And I told him I had plans to live there if my parents started fighting again, even though I didn't, really. And Dustin said if his new neighborhood sucked too bad he'd hitchhike back so we could both live there, maybe. I guess we made a bunch of plans like that, though.

And then we were quiet for a while and you could hear the cars headed somewhere up on Camelback Road. At one point some old friends of mine, I think it was Mickey and Foster, rode by on their bikes along the fence, but the trees were so thick there was no way they could see us in there.

"Nice fort," Dustin said. I was glad I showed it to him.

On our way back we kicked a few dirt clods in the water but it was kind of dumb, I guess. We really didn't want to go home, though, since we knew it was the last time we were going to see each other, probably. So we headed up to Circle to get a couple of Freezes and about halfway across this dirt lot, Dustin found a bunch of money again.

"Check it out!" Dustin said, holding up this five-dollar bill all covered in dirt. I must have walked right past it, too. And I swear it was like the third time it had happened.

There was that silver dollar and some other change he found when we were riding our bikes through the parking lot up at Tower Plaza Mall. And then I guess he found like eight bucks all wadded up on the ground near his locker at school that one time, but that was before I ever met him so I wasn't sure if it was true or not. But then he found that twenty in the candy aisle at Circle just a few weeks before all this, and I guess I walked right past that one also.

And I was trying to be happy for him, but I think he could tell I was kind of pissed after that. I mean, it was bad enough with all the cool stuff he had, but then to be finding money all the time, too. And now he was moving and even that sounded better. I mean, he'd have a whole new place to live, and a new school to go to, and no more *Greenwald* either ... And more girls would probably be there, and a bunch of new places to hang out, I mean ...

"Cool, where'd you *find* it?" I asked, as my voice cracked.

"Right there," he pointed. "You just kicked it when you walked past."

So I was the one that found it, actually. I mean, if you want to get technical about it. I didn't say anything, though. But I was still kind of pissed after that, and by the time we went home that day I didn't really care if he was leaving, to be honest. I mean, I did, I guess, but still.

Dustin was around for a couple more weeks anyway, getting ready to move with his parents. And we had already said goodbye when school got out, but instead of getting all sad and everything, we just made up a bunch of fake plans again. I mean, you kind of believe it's going to happen, so it's not like it's lying, really. But right before he left, I remember he called and wanted to hang out that one last time.

There was a carnival going on that night down at Kachina, which was the grade school we both went to before we transferred to Ingleside for seventh. And I was going down there anyway, so I just told him to meet me by the games they had set up near the dugouts. I remember I got there first, too, and it was just a bunch of grade-school kids around. I mean, it was the same carnival I went to every year but now it was just stupid.

So I rode around the field a few times, popped a couple half wheelies on the dork bike, and when Dustin showed up he must have felt the same way since he rode right past me towards the palm groves at the far end of the field. There was a neighborhood just beyond that, and right along the street we found a perfect spot to hide out and have a smoke behind one of those big, concrete irrigation wells. We could still hear the carnival going on, and with the lights shining down off the field everywhere, it made it seem a lot funner than it was, really. We leaned our pedals against the well so we could sit on our bikes, and after we lit a few smokes, Dustin started bragging about his new neighborhood again.

"It's all right, I guess ... Not many places to ride, though."

"Sounds cool," I said, as I stood on my bike and looked down in the well to try and change the subject. "Check it out," I said, as I flicked a few sparks down inside.

Dustin stood up next to me and took a drag and then coughed. "Camel, non-filters ... I stole them off my brother," he said, and we both laughed.

And we couldn't resist singing our old Christmas song after that, and I even made up a few new lines about my brother getting kicked out, so that was pretty funny. But all it did was remind me that Dustin was leaving the next day, and then he started bragging about his new house again so I spaced out for a while, I guess.

And some kids were playing out on the field under the lights, and it reminded me of those little guys jumping around in electric football. And then I was thinking of that stupid recess lady and how mean she was, and that time I stuck clay in her whistle. And the funny part was to go out past the line and watch her cheeks blow up when she tried to stop us, and then we'd be laughing, and we did it a couple times, so I guess I kind of got in trouble for it. And Dustin wasn't even around back then so he probably wouldn't even have cared that much. So then I started thinking about that time I won at Kill the Man, or, I lost, I guess, but depends on how you look at it.

Because Kill the Man was the greatest game we ever came up with back then, until they stopped us from doing it for some reason. I mean, it sounds pretty bad, and a few people got hurt, I guess, but let me just tell you how it went real quick:

So if you caught the red dodge ball, you were supposed to run with it for as long as you could while everybody else on the field tried to kill you. Or, you could just throw the ball up again real fast and watch somebody else get killed if you wanted. But there were so many kids trying to play all the time, so you barely got a chance at the ball ever. So when I caught it by accident that one day I just decided to run with it, and I guess I probably shouldn't have, though ...

Because at first I was thinking it was the biggest mistake I ever made, but then I dodged a couple of kids pretty easy, and then a few more after that, and I was able to break free and then I started running across the field dodging everybody. And so when nobody could catch me, I figured I won at that point, so I did a little victory dance, I guess. But that didn't go over so well, so some bigger kids from the grade above us came over and they started trying to kill me also. But those guys were even bigger than the last ones, so I could fake them out even easier, and that's when everybody started getting pissed, I guess, and you could hear they were all screaming, too.

"KILL HIM!! KILL HIM!!"

But why give it up now, I thought. I mean, if I was able to do it, why not keep going, right? So that's when I started running from one end of the field to the other, dodging and faking like you wouldn't believe, until it seemed like the whole school was after me.

"KILL HIM!! KILL HIM!! KILL HIM!! KILL HIM!!" *They all chanted it like they were out of their minds, too. And I swore I'd seen movies like that, where the whole town's chasing the guy with pitchforks and clubs and everything before they string him up and actually do kill him in the end. So I decided to throw the ball up after that so they could try to kill somebody else for a while, maybe, but that's when I realized it was too late anyway, since it wasn't the ball they were after anymore, it was me. And so all I could do was keep running and dodging and faking to save my life at that point. I mean, there was no escape, really. And I guess it never mattered if I had the ball or not, since they were going to kill me anyway. And so what the hell was the point to it all, I thought, and I still couldn't understand. So in a last-ditch, slow-motion fake, I held on to it—forever the king of Kill the—*

"So when school starts—you even listening?" Dustin asked.

"Yeah, sure," I said, as I flicked a few more sparks down into the well, still thinking about everything.

Dustin jumped down and left his bike against the well and went over and sat on the curb after that. And I took another drag but I felt kind of sick all a sudden, so I dropped what I had left in the water and went and sat down next to him. There were bugs flying everywhere, in and out of the streetlight above, and right as I sat down, this huge beetle flew over Dustin's head and landed on the sidewalk right across from us.

"It happened again, though." Dustin said, just as the beetle stopped moving all of a sudden.

"*Jesus*, look at that thing. *Gross*," I said, trying to change the subject. I mean, I knew what he was going to tell me anyway. Something about another stupid dream he had, probably. I really didn't want to hear about it, though, to be honest. And my sister's best friend Connie Buncle had just told me about how certain people like to make stuff up all the time just to get attention, so I figured that's why he was doing it. Like there's a certain kind of compulsive liar out there, she said, and my sister agreed with her, too.

But Connie Buncle was the same girl my cousin Smiley saw totally naked in the neighbor's pool that one day, so she was probably just mad he was telling people about it. And you can't blame her, really. But Smiley wasn't even smiling when he told us, though, since I guess the real thing was way different when you saw it up close. I mean, it wasn't like one of those half-covered, long-distance shots you always see in the magazines, is what he said.

He told us a lot more, too, so I was always nervous when my sister brought Buncle over since I couldn't stop thinking about it. The stuff she was saying about Dustin just trying to get attention all the time made a lot of sense, though.

But I guess you could say the same thing about Smiley, then. I mean, that he just made up the whole thing to get attention, probably. And maybe everybody was lying about everything all the time then, since you can't always see stuff when it happens, usually. And what was so bad about lying when you had to anyway, as long as it didn't hurt anyone, really. So if Dustin wanted to tell me another one of his stupid dream stories to feel better about himself, that was fine with me, I thought. I mean, he was moving right after that anyway.

"So what happened?" I asked, but Dustin got all quiet all of sudden.

"Look, he wants to hear it, too," I joked, since the beetle was still sitting there.

Then Dustin put his smoke out in a patch of dirt behind us and started telling me a bunch of weird stuff again.

"We were coming back from the new house," he said, "and I guess I fell asleep in the back of the car for a while, so it was like one of those daydreams, I think."

"*Jesus*, look at his shadow!" I said, still dwelling on the beetle. "It's like a buffalo ... He's a buffalo beetle!" I laughed, but I sounded like Radick all of sudden so I felt kind of stupid.

"It was just weird, though," Dustin said, "since he just said one thing this time."

"Every dream you have is weird," I said, and Buffalo Beetle started moving right then so I joked he didn't like the story.

"I know who it was, though." Dustin smiled a little. "It was that guy from that Sunday school thing we went to with Ludd that one time, remember?"

And I knew what he was talking about, even though I was trying to forget, since it was back when me and Ludd were still friends and he was still bothering me. But that was around the same time when me and Dustin first met and the whole thing was pretty stupid, I thought.

"You mean the asshole guy?" I said, and Dustin laughed.

"Yeah, I'm pretty sure it was him," he said. "He was a lot nicer in the dream, though."

But the guy wasn't nice at all, really, and I never wanted to be in that stupid church class in the first place. But Ludd's mom always made him go, so I ended up having to go with him a couple times, and that's when Dustin came with. And I was already going to church with my parents, but it was just for Christmas and Easter, like most people went, but I never liked being there since they always made you feel like you were going to hell for some reason.

And that asshole preacher guy from Ludd's class was even worse, though. I mean, he scared the crap out of me, to be honest. And all I did was ask him a question, really. Like if the story he was telling was true or not, since it didn't sound true at all. But that's when he freaked out and pulled me out of the class in front of everybody, and I got in a bunch of trouble after that since you're not supposed to ask anything, I guess. Anyway, Ludd's mom said I wasn't allowed to go anymore so I was glad it happened, actually.

"He was different in the dream, though," Dustin said, like he could hear me thinking again. "He just said one thing anyway. *TRAVERSE.*"

"Traverse? What an asshole." I said.

"My mom said it means like when you're climbing on the side of a mountain or something." Dustin said.

"I know what it *means*. What an asshole, though." I didn't really know what it meant back then, though.

What the asshole Sunday school teacher actually told Dustin in his dream:

"I can see now that my extreme religious beliefs are equal to the extreme position of having no belief at all ... just as my extreme nonbelief at times was a counter to my believing without question whatever I was told ... Although somewhere in the balance, I am connected through my spirit to something much greater than any preconceived idea I might have had before ...

For I can see this place I inhabit reach back through the infinite to its original, creative source, a source of creation that set in motion this system that now reaches out through the infinite ... And as a part of it all, my understanding comes through science, which defines our fundamental truth ... then on to evolve through the language of the spirit that will lead us beyond even the idea of me and you ...

But until then, I will follow this creative source from within ... I will listen to my subconscious through my dreams and pay attention ... I will do my best to recognize all outside synchronicities and connections, and with my conscience as a beacon, I will move toward growth and acceptance ... I will use my creativity as a form of prayer to the miraculous, as I shall honor my spirit before all other methods or dogmas.

And if we are honest about our place now in the journey, with our limited scientific definitions and still-primitive understandings of ourselves ... and if we are unable to climb in the direction of the summit as we once set out, then by all means ... ***TRAVERSE!"***

"And then it was just static after that," Dustin said, "like when the channels go off really late—"

"Oh, I love that thing right before it goes off the air, too, with the jets coming through the clouds and everything. '***And I reached out my hand ... and I touched the face ... of GOD.***'" I imitated the announcer as best I could, and Dustin knew what I was talking about, so he kind of imitated the guy along with me.

"But then my dad was listening to the radio," Dustin explained, "and I was just lying there in the back seat half awake, sort of, but then the static I was hearing in the dream started coming through the radio—"

Dustin stopped all of a sudden. "That's pretty much it, though."

And Dustin must have heard the noise before I did, since that's when Ares and those guys came riding up the street from behind us, yelling like crazy. And I think it was Mickey and Foster who were with him, and that older kid with the mustache they had buying beer for them, probably. But I know it was Radick for sure since he rode right up the sidewalk and ran over Buffalo Beetle right in front of us.

"*Sick. Look*, its guts are all *yellow*," he said as he circled back around to make sure he got him.

"*Why'd you do it?*" I asked, but Radick just laughed. I could tell Dustin wasn't happy either, since he went to go get his bike, so I followed him.

"What are *you* guys doing here *anyway*?" Ares asked.

"Just having a smoke," I muttered, still pissed about poor Buffalo.

Ares stopped his bike and popped his wheel up on the curb and started spinning it in place. "What's *your* story, *Essary*? I hear you're *moving*."

"Yeah, to Moon Valley. We're leaving tomorrow," Dustin said as he got on his bike and pushed off out into the street. I could tell he was ready to leave, too.

"*Moon Valley?*" the older kid said, like he knew the place was stupid or something, but Dustin just ignored him.

"How's the *dork bike*, McDonald?" Radick piped in as he circled back with another hyena laugh.

"I don't know ... *You still peein' the bed*?" I blurted, and I couldn't believe I said it, really. But that was the rumor from before, I guess, that Radick peed his bed till he was like eight years old or something. And I probably shouldn't have said it but I was sick of everybody making fun of the dork bike all the time, so I just said it anyway. Everybody laughed, too, and then Radick turned back and did a kick-out right in front of me so I knew it got him.

"Got a *smoke, McDonald*?" Ares asked, like we were good friends all of sudden.

"Uh ... *sure*, man." I felt kind of weird he was asking me, though.

And Dustin was already halfway up the street by that time, and I'm pretty sure he looked back to see if I was coming, but I didn't care, really. I mean, he was moving *anyway*.

Higher Than the Sun

Such a young man for a place like this
Well come on in, boy, see what it is
 you think you missed
This place is older than your life will be long

And everybody here knows what it is
 to not belong
And this is where I've always been
Where everything comes back again
So tell us what has brought you here

Could it be that, higher than the Sun
That is where the God you made
 will come from
But only if you do the things we say
Will you ever buy your way to heaven

It was more than one thing when
 it came to this
You think it was your choice
 but it's not a choice if you can't resist
And now you've got your rules
 for the bad from good
And here you help someone, because it's in your
  heart and you know you should
And this is where I've always been
Where everything comes back again and again
So tell us what has brought you here

Well could it be that, higher than the Sun
Well that is where the
 God you made will come from

But only if you do the things we say
Will you ever buy your way to heaven

Now that you're here don't be afraid
You can think of all the people that have
 probably felt this way
Within your conscience stands a fool
If there is a God why should it help you?

V

I can't believe I actually became friends with Ares after that. I mean, he was still being an asshole for the most part, but it was just different when you were around him. And Dustin was gone anyway, and the summer had just started, and I remember I got a new motocross bike right around that time, too, so all of sudden I was cool enough again.

And me and Ares even went out riding together that one day and ended up going by his grandma's house and got some of those awesome chocolate cookies she made. But then she started saying all this stuff, like what a good boy he was, so it was pretty funny. She wouldn't stop saying it, though, so Ares got all embarrassed and we ended up leaving before we even finished the milk she gave us. And I know I wasn't supposed to tell anyone, but it doesn't matter now, since I don't even live there.

And I only hung out with those guys for a couple weeks anyway, even though they ended up being pretty cool when you were friends with them, actually. I mean, I was kind of being a jerk myself back then, too, so I guess I didn't notice as much when they were being assholes.

But they were still doing all the same mean stuff as before: making fun of other kids on a regular basis, stealing stuff whenever they could, probably ... blowing up tailpipes and mailboxes with potatoes and M-80s, and they were always smoking pot, too, which I was sort of afraid of.

I mean, mainly since me and my cousin Smiley swore on a stack of Bibles back when we were ten years old that we were never going to do it no matter what. And we didn't even use a Bible when we said it either, so it probably didn't even count, really. We still swore on it, though.

But the main thing that scared me was that story my sister told me about how she took a couple of tokes off a joint that one time. But then it was laced with angel dust, and she didn't know it, I guess, so she freaked out and ended up waking up in the neighbor's front lawn the next day. A big patch of grass was missing right next to her, though, and she had grass in her mouth when she woke up, too, so she thinks she must've ate it, probably.

"You never know if it's laced," she'd say, so I was always afraid the same thing would happen to me if I ever tried it. And just the name of that other stuff scared the crap out of me, too. *Angel dust ... Jesus.*

But like I was saying, I was only in their stupid gang for a couple of weeks since Ares didn't think I was cool enough all of a sudden. And my new bike ended up getting ripped off right around that same time, so that didn't help. And that was the second one, too, and I swear I only left it out in front of Circle for like two seconds before some assholes stole it. I don't really want to talk about it, though. But Ares never did give me a hard time again. Probably afraid I'd bring up the stuff about his grandma or something.

But the summer got really boring after that. I mean, after doing all that stuff with Ares and those guys, since some of it was pretty fun, actually. And I guess I could have hung out with Radick or McKee since we were still friends, but I just decided to stick to myself for a while. I mean, I was sick of always trying to look cool anyway, and then with everybody always moving all the time, too. But I still had the dork bike and when I was alone I didn't have to worry about what anybody thought, really. I just liked riding it, though.

So I'd head out early, before it got too hot, ride along the canal and stop at the fort to have a smoke for a while. Then up to Thomas Mall to hang out around the department store fountains, maybe throw a few pennies in, see if there were any girls around. Then *play some pinball at the game room and not even worry if my bike got stolen, then back by the Shell station on 44th and Thomas to check if my tire might be leaking or if my brake was still broken. Then maybe I'd get a pop and a snack for the ride home, then head down along Thomas Road past the new Wagon Wheel shopping mall, but the place looked so stupid I never went in there before, then over to Tower Plaza to Yates Army Surplus, to maybe buy a canteen or some kind of captain's bar patch, but I usually didn't have enough. Then back down 36th Street to the fort again and have another smoke, and maybe listen to the radio and think about stuff before it was time to go home. And if I stood up while I was riding, I wouldn't burn my ass on the seat, and I could use my t-shirt to cover the handlebars so I didn't burn my hands too bad either, and then home in time for lunch so my mom was still happy, and then I'd probably just watch some reruns on TV ...*

Like maybe The Rat Patrol *or* Lost in Space *or* Hogan's Heroes, *or even* I Dream of Jeannie ... *or* Johnny Quest *or* Gilligan's Island, *or that episode of* Star Trek *where Captain Kirk fights that big lizard monster on the side of that mountain. Or maybe* Wild Wild West *or* The Rifleman, *or at least those were the shows I remember being on in the daytime back then—or even* The Jetsons *or* The Flintstones *or* Get Smart *were pretty funny, or then my sister might force me to watch* Hey, Hey, We're The Monkees, *or* The Partridge Family *was even worse, probably, or that new show* Kung Fu *that I really liked a lot, and ("Try to snatch the pebble from my hand, grasshoppa'.") And I'm sure I forgot some, but on and on it went till it finally cooled off enough to go out and ride my bike again.*

But then I really got bored, just being on my own like that. So I ended up hanging out with Radick and McKee off and on for the rest of the summer.

And we all got into skateboarding, so we went to High Roller a few times, which was the new skate park they had way up on 7th Street and Dunlap. But it was kind of the same thing with the board I had, though, since my parents got me this old Sims piece of crap.

But then I learned how to do an invert on the stupid thing, which was this new trick that none of my friends could do, at least. It's where you flip upside down and plant your hand on the coping to guide yourself back, sort of ... I mean, it's hard to explain, really, but at least everybody left me alone from then on.

And then we tried downhill skating for a while, but I only did it for about a week since my dad said I was going to kill myself, probably.

Like that time when me and McKee did that catamaran and got up to like sixty coming down that big hill at the end of 44th … Okay, we were only doing about thirty, maybe, but I remember that feeling, like we were going way too fast, and how McKee was giving me that freaked-out look all the way down, and I swore we were going to eat it near the end there, too, but then we made it somehow.

And then that story about that pro guy who was coming down 56th Street off the mountain, and I guess he was doing like eighty when he lost control and hit that big saguaro off the side of the road near the bottom there. And some older kids were there when it happened, too, so they told us all the details later; like how the guy's whole body was stuck up in the air on the side of that cactus, with all the needles going through his clothes and his pads, and how the paramedics were pulling all the stickers out of his face and his legs and hands one by one till they finally got him off the thing. I mean, the guy almost died, though, too, I guess. Anyway, we just stuck to street skating after that.

But that summer ended up being pretty cool after all. I mean, the best part was probably near the end when Radick took me with him to go see Peter Frampton at the coliseum since the guy he was going with backed out at the last minute. And I'd never been to a concert before and I wasn't even sure who Frampton was at first, till I heard a couple songs on the radio and realized I liked him already.

And my dad was supposed to take us, so me and Radick were waiting out in front of my house before we left, but that's when my brother came out to have a smoke and started saying a bunch of mean stuff about Frampton. And I think he was just there to talk to my parents that day or something, but I didn't even want to see him, really.

"Too bad you're in the nosebleeds," he said as he inspected our tickets and blew a bunch of smoke at us. And I wasn't even sure what he meant by it, really, just that our tickets sucked somehow. And then he acted like he was going to keep them for a second, but then he just threw them back at Radick.

"This guy *sucks anyway*," he said.

"*Shut up, Mike*," I blurted from under my breath as me and Radick walked across the lawn towards the driveway just to get away from him. And I didn't even think he heard me at first, but I guess he did since all of a sudden he got me in a headlock and started twisting my neck pretty bad.

"So what do *you* listen to, *man*?" Radick asked, like him and my brother were best friends all of a sudden.

"Yes," my brother responded, like we should know already. And he sounded like a snob with the smoke still in his mouth as he twisted my head down even further.

"Stop it, *man*!" I yelled, and I guess I was still trying to sound cool at that point, but at the same time I was hoping my mom could hear me.

"Say *YES IS THE BEST*," my brother insisted and he started to squeeze my head even harder.

And I knew what he meant by it, too, since Yes was this stupid band he always loved ... but they only had like one good song on the radio, though. *"I've seen all good people thunder heads this way so satisfied I monder way ..."* or whatever the stupid lyrics were. I mean, the guitar part in the beginning was pretty cool, I guess ... *DeeDeed'll DeeDeeDeeDeeDeeDee* ... or kind of like that. But he loved that stupid band so much, and he had all their albums, too, so he got all pissed if anybody ever said anything. I mean, their album covers *were* pretty cool, but what a stupid band name, though—*YES?*

"*NO!*" I yelled, thinking it was funny, but then he twisted my head so hard I almost blacked out, I remember.

"MOM!" I yelled, and I was yelling as loud as I could at that point, and I didn't even care how it sounded.

"SAY YES IS THE BEST," my brother demanded as he pinned me down in the dead grass near the edge of the driveway.

"SAY IT. SAY *YES IS THE BEST!*" he yelled. And with his face all twisted and the cigarette still in his mouth, he looked like some kind of Tasmanian asshole staring down at me.

"*YES SUCKS SHIT,*" I blurted, but I regretted it right afterwards, since that's when he started choking me pretty hard ... And I could hear Radick off to the side somewhere, laughing like crazy, and then I remembered how I was laughing the same way when Pat was choking him that one time ... And now I was sorry for everything I ever did or said to anybody, really, and I was trying to explain but nobody could hear me since my brother was choking me so hard ... And I really thought I was going to die at that point, too, but then he let go of me all of a sudden and I realized my dad had just come out. And, aw, man, was he going to pay for it. I mean, that son of a bitch was gonna pay for it now, I thought.

But my dad just walked right past us like nothing had even happened.

"You guys ready?" he asked.

And Radick was still laughing like crazy but he helped me get the dead grass off my back, at least. And as we pulled out of the driveway, I could see my brother standing over in the side yard with that stupid grin he always had since he knew he got away with it.

"YES SUCKS SHIT!" I yelled as loud as I could out the window as we drove off. Okay, I didn't, really. I wish I would have, though.

Anyway, then we were headed out of the neighborhood, and my dad never did say anything, either, and Radick was still laughing in the back seat, I remember. And my dad needed to stop and get some beer first, and then he was driving so slow the whole way we ended up being kind of late for the concert. And he was supposed to just let us out on the corner, I think, but he must have felt bad or something since then he pulled around all these barricades and ended up dropping us off right up near the entrance, somehow.

"When's this thing over?" he asked, and he sounded kind of pissed all of a sudden.

"It's like 11:30, Mr. McDonald," Radick said politely as we were getting out of the car to leave.

"*11:30? For Christ's sake*—just meet me here when it's done, then," he muttered, and I could see him lean back like he was going to sleep there, probably.

Then Radick just took off, so I followed him in between a bunch of semitrailers and barricades and then out into this big lot where they had all these railings set up to hold all the people back, I guess. But nobody was even there anymore, and it was too much to go back and forth the whole way, so we just went underneath them all so we could get there faster. And we still had to run up all these concrete steps to get up to the main entrance, but you could see how huge the place was, just looking up at it.

Some people were still out front when we got there so we got in line behind them, but that's when the cops grabbed this guy ahead of us and started asking him a bunch of questions.

"They're my tickets!" he was yelling, but they still pulled him off to the side somewhere. He looked kind of weird anyway, and he had this stupid hat on, like the *Beverly Hillbillies*, so it was pretty funny. But Radick just got all serious after that since they were searching people up ahead of us, I guess.

And then it was our turn, and the guy started searching me for some reason, and all I had was a pack of smokes, so I didn't think they'd even care about it, really. But then I was thinking that

Radick might have brought some weed or something, and so then I'd get busted for being with him, probably.

"You're not old enough to smoke," the guy said, as he grabbed the pack of Dorals I had hidden in my sock.

"Come on, *man*, don't even *worry* about it," Radick said, trying to convince the guy, I guess, and he sounded so cool when he said it I thought they were going to let us go for a second.

"Don't even worry about it, eh?" The guy smiled and then grabbed Radick all of a sudden and started pushing him around pretty hard while he was searching him. But something must have happened right then, since the guy got all distracted and started talking on his walkie-talkie and then he just let us go after that.

The whole thing was pretty stupid, I thought, and once we got far enough away, Radick pulled out a pack of Marlboros he had hidden in his underwear and started laughing.

"You don't put 'em in your sock, *man*," he said, like I was supposed to know already. Then he handed me a smoke, and I could see he had a couple joints in there, too.

From there we headed around the back of the building and everybody we showed our tickets to said we needed to keep going even farther. And you could hear there was a band playing already, even though Radick said the opening band always sucked anyway, but they finished right when we got to our seats, so we didn't even get to see them at all.

And then the lights came on, and I realized how far we were from the stage, and that's when Radick told me what my brother was saying, about us being up in the nosebleed seats, I mean. It was pretty stupid, though, I thought, because you never saw pilots getting nosebleeds, or people climbing mountains, either, so it didn't even make any sense, really. But everybody down on the stage looked like little ants crawling around, and some people even had binoculars sitting next to us, so I figured we wouldn't be able to see Frampton when he came out, either. And that's when I got kind of bummed, I guess, since our seats sucked so bad, and so my brother was right, probably. But Radick just kept looking around and telling me not to worry about it.

"Just follow me as soon as the lights go out," he said, and I kept asking him what he meant by it but he wouldn't tell me.

Then the crowed started yelling and everybody stood up so you could tell the show was going to start, and right when the lights went out, sure enough, Radick just took off.

"Follow me!" he yelled, but it was hard to at first, since we had to squeeze our way back through all the people in the aisle next to us. And everybody was yelling and smoking weed all of a sudden, too, but Radick just kept running. So I followed him back through the building the same way we came before, and then down a bunch of stairs where I almost lost him a few times since he wouldn't wait up for me ... And that's when we made our way out onto the main floor of the coliseum where people were going crazy everywhere. And I could barely see anything before we ended up right there in the second row, somehow ... And, *"Do you feel like I do?"* Frampton was singing with these weird tubes sticking out of his mouth, and everybody was screaming like crazy, and then all of a sudden this girl was standing there right next to me, but like really close, though, I mean ... And then another one was right next to her after that ... and that's when I realized they were everywhere, though ... like a thousand Connie Buncles all leaning up against us, drunk and stoned out of their minds, probably. And they were all throwing roses and stuff up on the stage at Frampton ... And you could tell they all loved music, too—and *I* loved music. Anyway, it was the greatest time I ever had in my life up until that point.

That's when everything started getting pretty messed up, though. And I should have known something was wrong when Dustin's mom called and wanted to talk to my mom first without them even telling me. And that was that morning when she stretched the phone cord all the way down the hall, and she was acting all weird when she came in my room, too, still talking with Dustin's mom.

"Timmy, you in there? Oh, there you are. It's Dustin's mother on the phone ... Yes, I was just going to tell him, Sharon. So ... we were thinking it would be nice if you were to go visit Dustin at their new house out in Moon Valley this weekend. Does that sound like fun?" she asked. I could tell she didn't expect me to answer, though.

"Okay, that sounds good," she said, as she wandered back and forth with the cord all stretched out. "I'll give the phone to Timmy then. Okay, that—that sounds good, okay. Thank you, Sharon ... okay, then ... okay ... you take care, now. Okay ... here he is, then ..."

And that's when she just handed me the phone while I was sitting there in bed, and at first I wouldn't take it, but she kept pushing it towards me. And I was trying to be quiet, like I wasn't there at all, and I was still kind of pissed since she kept calling me *Timmy* ... and thank you, *Sharon*?

What was *that* all about? Since she didn't even know Dustin's mom from before, and I hadn't even seen Dustin for the whole summer, and I already had a bunch of new friends anyway, and—

"Hey, *man*," I said.

"Hey," Dustin said.

"So, I guess I'm coming out there this weekend?"

"Yeah, me and my brother are supposed to pick you up this Friday."

"Okay, *cool*."

"Okay, see ya."

"Okay, *man*."

But that was it, though. Just really short like that, and then my mom took the phone back and acted like everything was fine then.

"This should be fun, don't you think?" my mom asked, as she held the phone under her chin and folded one of my shirts and put it in the dresser. "You can use your father's suitcase so you can bring some extra clothes and underwear."

"Okay," I said, as I got out of bed and I was kind of excited after that, actually. I mean, school was only a week away so I was surprised she was letting me go in the first place. But then she just stood there in the doorway before she left, and I thought she was going to tell me I had to clean my room again or something. She gave me this really sad look, though, I remember.

And the whole thing was pretty weird, I guess, but once I got dressed, I went out on my bike for a while and didn't really think about it too much. I mean, my parents are weird anyway, and I was looking forward to seeing Dustin, too, even though it was strange hearing his voice after so long.

So that next Friday afternoon I was watching from the front window when a tan car pulled up I'd never seen before, so I figured it was Dustin's brother, probably. And my parents had been arguing about something at the other end of the house, so instead of going back there I just yelled to my mom I was leaving. But I couldn't hear her say anything so I was stuck halfway out the front door with my bag against the screen since I knew I'd get in trouble if I just left like that.

"*MOM, I'M LEAVING,*" I yelled again, but like really loud this time, and I still couldn't tell if she heard me or not.

But right when Dustin's brother was coming up the walkway she started yelling a bunch of stuff back about me not forgetting extra underwear or something. *Jesus.*

"I GOT 'EM, I GOT 'EM!" I yelled.

And Dustin was still out in the car, so I was hoping he didn't hear anything, and his brother just smiled a little since he could tell I was embarrassed about it.

"*OKAY, BYE!*" I yelled, and shut the door behind me. I was just glad to get out of there, to be honest.

"So, you're Tim. I'm Matt." Dustin's brother shook my hand and helped me put my bag in the trunk. And I had never really met him before, since he was always away at school, I guess, but he was a lot nicer than I expected, considering all the mean stuff Dustin sang about him in that Christmas song we came up with. He had these stupid glasses on, though.

Anyway, as soon as I got in the back seat I knew Dustin must have heard what my mom was yelling, so we joked about me not having any extra underwear the whole way out of the neighborhood after that. It was pretty stupid, though, I thought.

Then me and Dustin started talking about other stuff, and it was weird because we just went back to being best friends again, somehow. I mean, it was like he never left in a way. I could tell he was pissed about something, though. Probably since his new neighborhood sucked so bad, or at least that's what I was thinking anyway. But I remember we stopped talking for a while after that.

And then we were driving up Camelback Road, past all the department stores on 24th Street, and we were a lot farther than I ever went with my dad, usually. And it felt great just knowing I was getting away for the weekend to somewhere I'd never been before. And I even felt a lot older, for some reason, like I was a lot more confident, I guess, and I wasn't even really that scared anymore, I don't think. And then Matt started playing some cool music on the radio, and then he flipped through some channels till one of my favorite songs came on, and "Goodbye Yellow Brick Road." And I wasn't really sure what the lyrics meant at all, but the sound of the music and the words were changing along with everything outside as we drove ... I mean, like everything was changing along with the music, somehow ... And then I was thinking about how upset Dustin must have been for having to move so far away in the first place, and he probably wasn't able to find any new friends as good as us, either. And if I was him, I'd be trying to find my way back to the way it was before, somehow ... And Matt was probably thinking about something really smart, and feeling pretty great since he could do whatever he wanted, probably. I mean, since he had his own car and everything. And then I was thinking back through all the things I had done that summer, and about all the stuff I wanted to tell Dustin when I had a chance to later. But I didn't want to piss him off, though, either, because he still seemed kind of upset about something. And it was probably because his new neighborhood sucked so bad, is what I was thinking. I figured I better not even mention it, though. And the farther we drove, the more everything changed, but I guess it kind of stayed the same in a way, too ... And we kept passing 7-11s instead of Circle Ks, so I wasn't sure what that was about either. And then we even passed High Roller Skate Park, way up on 7th Street and Dunlap, where I only got to go a few times that summer since my dad said it was way too far ... And so why were they letting me go so far to see Dustin then, I thought, and "What do you think you'll do then, there's nobody left to blame? It'll take you a couple of Vikerin tablets, and we can never meet again ..." *And I didn't really know what Vikerin tablets were — and I still don't, really — but they sounded pretty cool so I pretended I knew anyway. And then we passed one of those big churches with a bunch of people standing out front, and it made me think of those classes I went to with Ludd, and all the churches I had been to for the holidays before that ... And maybe everybody had questions about stuff, but they were just going along with it so they didn't have to go to hell like I was, probably. And it reminded me of that asshole preacher guy again, and how he showed up in Dustin's dream after that, and maybe it was the same thing for him, too, and—*

Just then Matt turned the radio down and I realized another song was on: *"Momma's got a squeeze box, daddy never sleeps at night ... "* and I wasn't really sure what that meant, either. It sounded pretty stupid, though, I thought. I mean, I still hate that song. Then some commercial came on after that, something about Oscar Mayer wieners, so Dustin turned it down all the way.

"Here's Moon Valley coming up," Matt said. "It's just up here to the right."

I'm never going to remember, I thought, and then I guess I said it out loud, too.

"Just remember it's the first road you come to when you get to the other side of this hill," Matt said, as we headed over the mountain.

Then Matt turned the radio back up, but there was still a commercial on, and then Dustin said something but I couldn't hear him too well, and then Matt said something back and they both started laughing, so I guess Dustin was fine then.

"Why you guys laughing?" I asked, as I leaned over the front seat, but Dustin said it was nothing and that he'd just tell me later. I hate it when people say that, though, since I always get the feeling they're laughing at me, probably. And then you bring it up later and they always say they can't remember, so you know it was about you anyway.

Then we turned down some street, but I wasn't really paying attention too much, after being laughed at, I mean. But I could see right away that the place was way better than the old neighborhood. I mean, all the houses were really big, like the ones we used to hang out around near the mountain, and then the street curved around and you could see all the trees and flowers and rocks in the yards everywhere. I mean, like one of those really nice parks up near my mom's work in Scottsdale. *Snottsdale* is what we used to call it.

Anyway, it was almost dark by the time we got there, and as we pulled up the driveway, there were a bunch of lights above the garage and along the backyard fence shining down on us, like in that movie *The Great Escape* or something. And now I was stuck there the whole weekend, I thought, in this stupid rich house with everybody laughing at me, probably.

As we got out of the car, Dustin leaned out into the driveway on a pair of crutches since his leg was all messed up and he never told me.

"I ate it on my bike pretty bad … I'll just tell you later," he said, before I even had a chance to ask anything. And I could see he had his pant leg cut down the sides with a big padded cast underneath, too.

"So you made it, Tim!" I could hear Ms. Essary's voice from behind the lights. I was still kind of pissed at her for talking to my mom, though.

Dustin's new house was kind of ridiculous if you ask me. I mean, it was way bigger than his old one, or my house, or anywhere I'd ever been before, really. And that was just the impression you got as you walked around from the front driveway. But right when you looked inside, you could see all the way across the living room and out these big back windows, and they had a pool and Jacuzzi in the backyard, too.

"My room's this way," Dustin said, as he crutched his way past me through the front door. I guess he could see the look on my face. "I'll show you the rest later," he added, and then he just acted like it was no big deal.

Ms. Essary was still out front talking with Matt about something and then she called after us that dinner was going to be ready soon.

"Okay!" Dustin yelled back to her as I followed him into this big open room full of really nice furniture with a bunch of cool pictures of trees and stuff they had hanging up everywhere.

Dustin's dad was on the other side of the room sitting in this big chair reading something, but he didn't look up or even say anything. I mean, I had only met him a few times before and he hardly ever said anything then either. Then Dustin stopped for a second like he might introduce us again, but then just nodded for me to follow him into the next room.

From there we went down this long hallway where you could barely see anything since there were just a few small lights along the bottom of the wall, and all I kept thinking was how scary it was going to be to try to find the bathroom late at night. And then I was thinking about all the cool stuff Dustin had before, and how his new room was going to be even bigger this time, and then he'd have a bunch of new stuff in there, probably, too.

But when we got to his room there was hardly anything in it, really. I mean, it was a lot bigger, I guess, and he had the same bed and dresser and a few chairs, but all his cool stuff was gone, though, it looked like. His old *Star Wars* poster was on the wall across from his bed, and he had a few game boxes on the dresser, but that was it, really. I mean, I almost thought it was a spare bedroom they wanted me to stay in at first, till I saw Pecker was still there in his cage over in the corner.

"*PECKER!*" I yelled. I was kind of glad to see him, actually.

Dustin laughed a little as he leaned against the dresser with his crutches and emptied some change from his pockets. I was still looking around the room for the rest of his stuff, though, and then I was kind of pissed he didn't have anything, to be honest.

"I haven't even been here much because of my leg and everything," he said. Then he pointed with one of his crutches across the room towards a window where you could see the pool outside with a bunch of lights shining up everywhere.

"You can put your bag over there," he said. "We got a mattress you can use, too."

"Okay, *cool*," I said, as I set my bag against the wall. "But what happened, though … I mean, where is everything?" I asked, as I started going down the list. "Like your GI Joes, your models, your light sabe—"

"Most of it's still packed from since we moved," Dustin said, but then he seemed like he was getting pissed again and I realized I should have just asked him about his leg, probably.

"I'll just tell you about everything later," he said, "We're supposed to go eat anyway." Then he leaned onto his crutches and limped his way past me towards the door. I took another look around before we left, too.

"*PECKER!*" I yelled again. I felt kind of stupid when I said it, though.

Ms. Essary had a couple TV dinners waiting for us in the living room, and instead of the stupid kids meals my mom always got, you could see right away these were Hungry Mans. I mean, it's what my dad and brother always ate, and the desserts were a lot bigger so you could tell. And his mom even had us set up on the couch with a couple trays so we could watch TV while we were eating, too. And that's how it should be, I thought, where everybody could eat a Hungry Man dinner if they wanted, and even watch a little TV while they were eating it, not be stuck at some stupid dinner table with everybody arguing since nobody wants to be there in the first place. And if you want to have a Coke with your dinner instead of having milk all the time, well, that was fine also. And even if you spill a little Coke on the carpet next to the couch it was no big deal, either. Actually it was, though, I guess, since Dustin said his mom was going to freak out if she saw it, so I ran and got a towel from their bathroom and I was able to clean it up before she saw anything. But besides all that, the dinner we had was awesome. We both got the Salisbury steak ones with the apple cobbler dessert and watched *Wonder Woman* at the same time. Then the *Incredible Hulk* was on, so we watched that up to the point where the guy freaks out and starts smashing everything. I was really starting to like it there too.

But then we went back to Dustin's room and he basically told me everything: about how he didn't really crash his bike like he told me, but that he had gotten really sick ever since he moved.

"I got cancer," he said, and I'll never forget the look he gave me. Like he already knew it was over, probably. And I guess I said I was sorry at that point, or some stupid comment like that, but then I just remember feeling like I couldn't say anything, really. Like with my parents that time when I couldn't warn them about the fire, maybe. And it wasn't like I even knew what cancer was, really. Just that if you got it you were going to die from it, is what I heard.

And at some point I must have sat down in one of the chairs across from Dustin, who was leaning against the bed with his leg all propped up. And then he was undoing the Velcro straps of his cast since I guess he wanted to show me what happened. And I think I tried explaining that I didn't need to see it, really, but he still wanted to show me, I guess. But that's when I could see the huge cuts down both sides of his leg, like all the way down to his ankle. It was the grossest thing I ever saw in my life, too. And there weren't even any stitches, either, since I guess the cuts were so big they used these big metal staples to hold the skin together, is what he told me.

"They put a new bone in my leg," Dustin said, like he was kind of proud of it. Then he moved the padding off to the side so I could see how far the staples went down. And I think I just nodded at that point and made some stupid face, probably, but I guess he could see I was freaking out about it.

"They got the bone from a guy that died already," Dustin said.

Right then Ms. Essary came in, and I was glad she did, too. I mean, I could barely handle what he told me about having cancer, let alone the stuff about having a dead man's bone in his leg. *Jesus.*

"Here, you can use these, Tim," Ms. Essary said, as she put a handful of sheets and a pillow on the dresser. "Matt's bringing in an extra mattress in a minute," she added, and then gave me a sad look.

"So you told him?" she asked Dustin.

"Pretty much." Dustin said, as he was putting the straps on his cast back in place.

Then Ms. Essary seemed kind of upset at that point and started to restack the sheets on the dresser. "Well, Tim, your mother and I just felt it was best if Dustin told you himself, so I hope you can understand. It's been very hard for Dustin these last few months, but he's been so glad to know you were coming—"

"*Mom*," Dustin interrupted.

"That's okay," I said, surprised I was able to speak again. "I can understand." I couldn't, though, really.

"Okay, well ... that's good then ... Do you guys want to go in the Jacuzzi?" Ms. Essary asked, but it didn't sound like she cared what our answer was. "Dustin usually goes in the evenings since it helps him feel better. I'll get you boys some towels then," she added, as she went out into the hallway. And then we were both just sitting there really quiet, so it was kind of uncomfortable at that point.

"I THINK DUSTIN HAS SOME OLD SWIM TRUNKS YOU CAN USE IF YOU DON'T HAVE ANYTHING, TIM!" Ms. Essary called from the hallway.

"TIM BROUGHT EXTRA UNDERWEAR!" Dustin yelled back, and laughed, but I don't think his mom heard it since she didn't say anything.

"Real funny, man," I said, even though I thought it was pretty stupid. I was just glad we were joking around again, though.

Then Matt came in with the extra mattress and put it on the floor next to the window. He gave me the same sad look his mom did, too, I guess to see if Dustin had told me yet. Then Ms. Essary came back with a few pool towels and put them on the edge of Dustin's bed, and then went about setting up the extra mattress on the floor for me. But nobody was saying anything and it got really uncomfortable, until Matt let Pecker out of his cage and put him on his shoulder and started walking around pretending he was a pirate, so it was pretty funny.

"*Arrrggg ... Hey, Dustin, you need to let your PECKER out more often*!" he said, which made us laugh really hard, except for Ms. Essary.

"There ... your bed's all ready, Tim," she said as she finished straightening out the sheets. Then she started to leave so we stopped laughing.

"Dustin, it's going to be time for your treatment soon," she said, as she was standing in the doorway giving us all this serious look. "You guys can go in the Jacuzzi for now, but have Matt help you with it later, okay, honey?"

"Okay, mom," Dustin said.

"I'll help him," Matt said with a grin as he put Pecker back in his cage.

Treatment, I thought, as I looked at Dustin.

"I'll just tell you later," he said.

Matt said he'd go in the Jacuzzi with us, so it helped to lighten things up a little, since even though I felt like I could talk again, I still didn't know what to say, really. I mean, I had never known anybody who had cancer, and the closest thing I could think of was *The Boy in the Plastic Bubble* or something. I mean, I knew it was way different, and that movie seemed kind of stupid now anyway, so I didn't bring it up at all.

And I ended up borrowing a pair of Dustin's old swim trunks like his mom said, but they were way too big for me and they had all these weird stripes so I was pretty embarrassed when I walked out to the Jacuzzi. The backyard was a trip the way they had it all set up, though. There were a bunch of palm trees and plants all around, and the Jacuzzi was higher up so you could look out over the pool with all the lights everywhere. You could even see over the backyard fence that they had a golf course back there, too.

Matt turned the bubbles on for the Jacuzzi while Dustin took his cast off again, but it took him a while to get in the water since he had to ease his leg in real slow. Once Dustin was in, me and Matt got in, and it was hotter than hell, too.

"Since Tim knows everything now, maybe he can be a part of your session later," Matt said, smiling at Dustin as he settled in the water across from us.

Dustin smiled a little as he sunk down in the water the rest of the way, but he didn't say anything.

But that's when Matt started telling me about chemotherapy and all the treatments Dustin had to have. He said it was like some kind of radiation crap that made you really sick before it ever helped you, though. And then he was saying something about smoking pot, too, and I thought he was just joking at first. But he kept going on about how all these doctors were saying that smoking it was a way to help people so they wouldn't get sick from using chemotherapy, and so that's why Dustin needed it.

"You can try it with us if you want," Dustin said.

But all I could think of was how I swore on a stack of Bibles with my cousin that time, and how Rocky never did it, probably, and then how my sister ended up eating half the neighbor's front lawn, since you never know if it's angel dust either.

"You guys go ahead, *I'm fine, man*," I said, and I was trying to sound as cool as possible, but I knew I sounded stupid when I said it. And then I felt really embarrassed right then so I went under the water to try to change the subject.

And that's when I realized I could stay down there for a really long time if I wanted—I mean, since the water was so warm, I guess … So I just sat there slumped over face down, floating down in the bubbles and just thought about everything for a while … And it felt great just floating down there, too, like I didn't have to worry about anything, really… And that's when I started to think that maybe it wouldn't be so bad if I smoked a little weed after all … I mean, if it helped Dustin to feel better, like they said … And all my other friends had already done it, and now my best friend had cancer and was probably going to die soon, and what an asshole I'd be if I didn't try it with him … But I was starting to need air again so I decided right then, before I came back up, I was going to do it …

I could hear Matt laughing through the water as I stood up. "We thought you were going to stay down there," he said.

"I'll try some," I said, all out of breath.

"Cool, man, it's no big deal, really," Matt said, "You probably won't even feel it the first time."

But that's what everybody always said. I mean, that you probably won't even feel anything the first time. It always sounded like a trick to me, though, since just the idea that you won't feel anything makes you want to try it just to see if you will. So then it's like your first time isn't really your first time either, since you're not supposed to feel anything anyway—which makes your second time (when you're supposed to feel something) actually your first time, but by that time, it's no big deal since you've already tried it, right? I mean, I was still going to do it. I just knew it was a trick when people said it, though.

"So, did you feel anything when you first did it? I asked Dustin, trying to prove my point.

Matt laughed. "I don't even remember the first time."

Dustin thought for a second. "Yeah ... I felt better, I think."

Exactly, I thought. But I don't know what I thought, really.

"You'll probably like it, though," Dustin added, and I could tell he was happy I was going to try it with him.

We stayed out back a little longer, and I even jumped in the big pool for a second just to see what it was like. It was way too cold, though, so I got back in the Jacuzzi pretty quick. Then Dustin said he had had enough, so Matt helped him out of the water. Once we dried off, Matt said he'd meet us back in Dustin's room in a few minutes, so we went back there to wait for him.

Then Ms. Essary came by Dustin's room to talk to us before Matt got there and started saying a bunch of stuff. Like if anybody else was going to try it, then she didn't want to know about it. Then Dustin told her nobody else was going to do anything anyway, but that even if they did, nobody would say anything about it later. They both kept looking at me, too, which made me really uncomfortable since I knew I liked telling people stuff.

Once his mom left, though, Dustin gave me this serious look. "We couldn't get it from the doctor, so my brother gets it from this guy. Just don't tell anyone," he said, so I swore I wouldn't.

But that's when Matt came in with this big ol' bag of weed and this huge, red, plastic tube thingy, which was a bong, but I didn't know it back then. And to be honest, I had only seen people smoking joints and pipes up until that point, so the bong thing was kind of intimidating. But Matt showed me how to work it, and my first time I did it perfect, too, he said, even though I coughed pretty bad right afterwards. And Dustin had already gone before me and it seemed like he knew what he was doing pretty well. And then it was Matt's turn and you could tell right away he was like a pro at it or something. But then we all just sat there in a circle on the carpet in Dustin's room and took turns taking puffs from the big, red bong, and none of us really said much after that.

And that's when I started thinking about everything, and it was just hard to believe what Dustin had told me. Then Matt and Dustin started talking about something, but I didn't pay too much attention until Matt said he had to leave.

"*Have fun*," he said, and then gave us a big grin before he closed the door.

Dustin gave me a strange look. "You feel anything?" he asked.

"*No* ... I thought I wasn't supposed to feel anything the first time," I said, but Dustin just laughed.

So then we just sat there for a while, and Dustin started messing with his cast, and that's when I started thinking again, and everything seemed really clear all of a sudden: about all the stupid dreams he had had, and the strange way he was acting before he moved and everything, and even all the money he had found back then might have been part of it, somehow ... But now he was probably dying and it reminded me of when I was thinking about how far the universe went ... and that maybe it was kind of like the same thing then, since when you die you're supposed to be gone forever ... and, in a way, we were already gone forever before we even got here, so maybe we're just gone forever again, somehow ...

It was too scary to think about, though, so I started looking around the room till I noticed Pecker looked really strange for some reason, just sitting there in his cage all alone ... And just the idea that he was in a cage in the first place seemed really stupid ... and what if animals were free and *we* were the ones in cages, and maybe we were already in cages but we just couldn't see it yet ... *and maybe we were already in like these invisible cages but we just couldn't see it!* Okay, I was stoned.

Then Dustin started laughing since I must have looked pretty funny trying to figure it all out. So I told him everything I was thinking. I mean, all the stuff about how we were in cages anyway, and he thought it sounded right to him, too. But then it got really quiet all of a sudden, so we started laughing about that for a while.

And Dustin wanted me sneak out into the kitchen and get us some chips and soda and stuff since we were both pretty hungry again, but I told him there was no way I could do it since I'd probably get lost if I tried. But that made us start laughing again, and then we started whispering for some reason. Then Dustin ended up limping out into the hall on his crutches saying he was going to do it himself, and I couldn't stop laughing about that either. He came back with some stuff to eat, though, and we both sat in our beds and ate Fritos and split a soda until Dustin said he was feeling really tired and that he needed to go to bed.

But that's when he really freaked me out, and he made me promise not to laugh at first, but he basically pulled all the hair off his head and threw it on the dresser. It looked like one of those tribbles from *Star Trek* when it landed, too. And I guess it was a wig or something he had been wearing the whole time but never told me. He was totally bald, though.

"I lost all my hair from the chemo," he said, as he leaned forward and rubbed his head all around to show me.

And I didn't know what to say again, really, but then I thought of something real quick.

"It looks so real, though ... I mean, I didn't even notice." I was serious, too.

"Yeah, my mom had it made for me," Dustin said, but then he seemed kind of upset again.

And that's when I got upset at myself, too, because I started to feel like I was going to laugh at him for being bald or something. And what an asshole that would be, to be laughing at my best friend who was not only probably going to die soon, but who had just lost all his hair from using some other crap that made him feel even worse. I still couldn't help it, though, and I guess he could tell, since then he just started laughing right along with me after that.

And then the lights were out, and nothing was funny anymore, and I remember the shadows floating across the ceiling and it scared the living crap out of me till I finally fell asleep.

And I guess I had my own stupid dream that night, too. Something about a little dog coming in and nudging me on the back of the neck, trying to wake me up for like an hour. And I wasn't even sure if I was dreaming at first, since it seemed so real, and I didn't think the Essarys even had a dog so it kind of freaked me out a little. Then all of a sudden the dog was gone, and it was like Pecker got out of his cage somehow and was flying around the room in the dark like crazy. He even dive-bombed me a couple of times and then flew straight out the window in the end, so I knew I was dreaming at that point.

But when we got up the next day, I realized I better not say anything about having a dream with Pecker flying around unless I wanted to hear a bunch of Pecker jokes from then on. I mean, not from Dustin, probably, but from Matt for sure. Like, maybe Pecker landed on my shoulder all night or something stupid like that. And he actually did land on my shoulder a couple of times—in the dream, I mean. See, now I got you thinking it.

But I did tell Dustin about the dog in my dream since it seemed so real, but he swore they didn't have one. And then he said I was probably one of those cases of people smoking weed, where they not only felt it the first time but they also hallucinated a bunch of stuff somehow, too. I didn't believe him, though, but I guess Matt said it happened to a friend of his.

Anyway, that next morning was just weird altogether since I couldn't stop thinking about everything Dustin had told me. And for a second I was thinking maybe it never happened somehow. But after we got up and we were getting ready, I could see his leg was still messed up, and his hair was still gone, too, and then his mom came in his room talking about a bunch of stuff and gave him some medicine. And I had a lot of questions, I remember, but it just didn't feel right to ask him anything.

Then Ms. Essary said she was going out for a while, so me and Dustin went to the kitchen and heated up a couple Pop-Tarts for breakfast. They only had the sprinkled ones, though, so they sucked pretty bad, and I was going to mention how my mom always got the cinnamon kind since they were a lot better, but I figured he didn't want to hear about it.

After we had a couple of bites, I carried the rest for us in a paper towel. Dustin wanted to go outside and he couldn't carry anything with his crutches. It was already getting hot out, too, but there was a bench they had set up under some trees in the front yard so we went and sat there in the shade for a while.

And I hadn't really seen anything out front the day before since it was pretty dark when we got there, but now I could see they were in a cul-de-sac with some other rich houses around, and across the street there was a baseball field with a playground next to it. Dustin said it was the new middle school he was supposed to go to before he got sick. We both only had one more year before high school, too.

After we finished our Pop-Tarts, I went and drug the hose over so we could get a drink.

Dustin said I had to wind it back up, though, since his dad would get all pissed if it was still lying there.

Then Dustin wanted to go over to the school for a while. On the way there he showed me how fast he could go on his crutches. There was nothing really to do when we got there, though, so we just ended up sitting on the swings after that. I offered him a smoke but he didn't want it.

And then neither one of us were saying anything, and it reminded me of that time on the canal when he had just told me he was moving, like some weird conversation was going on without us again. And then I just felt really uncomfortable for some reason, so I said something I wish I wouldn't have, really.

"So ... you meet any girls this summer?" I asked, and I realized right away how stupid it was to say it. And Dustin just looked away but I could tell he thought it was stupid, too.

"Sorry, man," I said. "It's just hard to believe what happened ... I mean ... maybe the doctors can do something," I added, trying to sound optimistic.

Then Dustin got up from the swing and dug his crutches around in the sand, like he made his mind up about something. "I'll be alright," he said, and he kind of smiled a little.

I could tell he didn't mean it, though. Or even if he did, it was in some stupid way, probably, like he'd be all right even if he died, or something weird like that.

"They should be able to help, though," I said, trying to convince him as I followed him back out towards the road, but he didn't say anything and I wasn't even sure if I believed it.

And as we headed back along the sidewalk towards his house, is when it hit me what a great friend he was. I mean, always going along with all the stupid shit I said, or not saying anything when he knew I was jealous about something, or even when I was lying, probably ... or even when I was hanging out with assholes instead of him. And now he was probably dying of cancer, and I just went and said something so stupid again, and he was still being nice for some reason.

When we got back to his house, his mom was waiting for us in the driveway and said I had to go home early. Something about how Dustin needed to get his rest since he was going to the doctor's early on Monday, and that it was probably better if Matt just took me home that afternoon instead of me staying another night. But I think she just found out about us bringing food in his room and got all upset about it. I didn't even do it, though.

But I was kind of all right with it, to be honest, since I didn't know what we were going to do for another whole night anyway—except maybe smoke some more weed, but I didn't really feel like doing that again so fast. I've done it a bunch of times since then, though.

We still had a couple hours before Matt could take me home, so we went back to Dustin's room to wait till then.

"How about another game?" he said as he pulled a chess set out from the stack of boxes on the dresser. Dustin was the one who showed me how to play when we first met, too. I was really bad at it, though, and he let me win a bunch of times, I remember.

"Okay, but really try this time," I joked, and he swore he would.

But as we were pulling the chairs over to the edge of the dresser, I could see he was having a hard time with his crutches again, and I just started feeling really bad for him at that point—and so maybe I should be the one to let *him* win this time, I thought. But as soon as we started playing I realized something: that if we were both trying as hard as we could to let each other win, then it was still like some weird, backwards competition, in a way. Like whoever loses, wins, or something strange like that. So the whole way through I kept thinking of how bad I needed to play in order to lose this time, or to win, I mean. And I swear I played the worst game you could ever imagine, on purpose, and I still lost—or won, I guess. He just left his queen sitting there, so I had to take it.

Dustin came with us when Matt took me home, and we drove back the same way we came the day before. But I barely remember the drive this time, or the music that was on, or even if we talked at all, just that it felt really uncomfortable the whole way. And then we were there already, driving up Camelback Road almost to 44th, back at the same place we had been friends for so long. And I remember thinking how everything looked the same, too, for some reason, like nothing had even happened, maybe. And then I just wanted to get it over with, to be honest. I mean, saying goodbye and everything.

"You can just drop me off here," I said, and I could feel my throat getting all tight.

"You sure?" Matt said, as he started to slow down. "I can take you right to your house if you want."

"It's alright, *man*. I'll just walk from here," I insisted, and as I grabbed my bag I started crying a little, I guess. I was pretty sure they couldn't tell, though.

"Maybe you can stay over again in a couple weeks," Dustin said, as Matt pulled over to the curb. We were right there at the entrance to his old complex, too.

"Yeah, sure," I said, without thinking, "I can probably do it." But I knew I was lying at that point, and I knew he could tell, too.

But that's when Dustin reached over the front seat and shook my hand, and there was this look he gave me, like he knew it was the last time we were going to see each other, probably.

"Everything'll be alright," he said, and he could see I was crying as I stepped out onto the curb, and with the sound of the traffic, I could barely speak again.

"okay," I choked. "i'll call ya."

But school started a week later, and Pam Athena was in my new home room, only two seats away, I might add, and Radick and McKee were in a few of my classes, and Greenwald was on my ass again, and, no, I never did call him.

And even though I told everybody who would listen about Dustin having cancer, and the dead man's bone in his leg, and the weed we smoked, and the dream I had (about the dog part, anyway), I still just figured he was going be alright somehow.

But then a month had gone by, and I still hadn't heard anything, and I still hadn't called since I was afraid to, I guess, but that's when I got a bad feeling, though.

So when the phone rang early that Saturday, and through the door in my room I could hear my mom answer it in the kitchen. And then her voice changed all of a sudden so I knew something must have happened. But I was afraid to go out there, so I used a trick I figured out where I could listen in on the phone really quiet. I mean, so nobody would know I was there, really, but that's when I could hear it was Ms. Essary crying.

"Dustin died," she said, and then my mom was telling her how sorry she was. And I was still there listening in the background, stunned, since I couldn't believe it, really.

"We just wanted you to let Tim know," Ms. Essary said, finally, and I thought I should probably say something but I just hung up really quiet after that. Because that's when I got the most horrible feeling you could ever imagine, like if every bad thing I ever worried about since the day I was born just all of sudden happened at once, somehow. And then I was crying again, too, I guess, but like really hard this time, like when you can barely breathe since it feels like you just got the wind knocked out of you. And I felt really stupid, too, since I knew I was supposed to *take it like a man*, like people said, I guess, but I just couldn't help it.

And then my mom came in my room to try to tell me what had happened, but I guess she could see I knew already. And I thought I was in trouble for listening in on the phone when I wasn't supposed to, but then she just gave me a hug instead. And it felt really good, too. I mean, at first anyway, but then I just felt embarrassed, so she left me alone in my room after that.

But then I just couldn't stop thinking about it, about like how was it even possible? That we were just best friends a few weeks before, talking and hanging out and everything, and then all of a sudden he was just gone like that—but like forever, though. And it was the same kind of stuff that scared the crap out of me before, about the universe going on and on the same way, so this made me even more scared.

And how could somebody die when they're only thirteen, too? Because I was only thirteen, so that meant the same thing could happen to me at any second. And what was the point in being friends with anybody then either, if this is how it was going to end up?

I was still trying to understand as I walked out front, but it felt a lot better out in the sun, at least.

And then I was just standing there in the side yard, staring at the dead grass, and, yeah, I was still crying a little, off and on, I guess. But that's when I got the feeling like I needed to get out of there for some reason. So I grabbed the couple smokes I had left in my stash and ran as fast as I could down the alley and along the canal till I got to the orchard since I figured I'd just hide out in my fort for a while.

A couple people were riding their bikes past when I got there, so I just pretended I was skimming rocks at first. I needed to catch my breath anyway, and then I used my shirt to wipe my face off a little since I knew I looked stupid from crying so much.

Once they were gone, I snuck down the bank into the trees and when I got in my fort is when I realized somebody had been in there. A bunch of stuff was moved around and my bucket was gone, and there were even some butts put out on the plywood floor, too, the fucking assholes. *Jesus.* And now I was saying the Lord's name in vain again, so I was sure I was going to hell for that, and I figured I'd know what going to hell was like soon anyway, since I was probably going to die at any minute. And I couldn't even go to my fort anymore since somebody else had found it. And there was nothing I could do to bring Dustin back, and I knew I couldn't stop anybody else from dying from then on either.

And so that's when I just gave up, really. I made a spot to sit down on a piece of cardboard and just leaned up against the tree in the middle. I tried to have a smoke, but then I felt like I was going to throw up all of a sudden so I just put it out. I put it out right in the same spot the assholes did, too.

And then I could hear the cars driving by up on Camelback Road, and it reminded me of when I was there before, just listening to music all those times and thinking about everything ... and the wind was coming in through the branches all around, and the trees were kind of moving outside so it looked different ... and then I was just sitting there, noticing everything around ... like when you're not even thinking at all, sometimes, just listening ...

For the Death of Dustin Essary

All the lullabies never called my name
And worry never solved, never solved anything

And the heart of any lie is when it's spoken
And the truth of any lie
 is when it's someday learned from

So I lie till I believe
I'm the only one who's jealous
Of the riches that were stolen from me
Everybody dies
Am I the only one who's nervous
For the life they're going to bleed from me

All the stories told never showed you the way
I never once was wrong, I never once was afraid

And the heart of any lie is when it's spoken
The truth of any lie I could someday learn from

So I lie till I believe
I'm the only one who's honest
Of the truth I've yet to face in me
Everybody dies
Am I the only one who's nervous
Because nothing's going to save me

Well I must have played a victim to the world
Justified it all so many times before
Because the mind will think it's best
 to take control
Though the master is my soul

So I lie till I believe
I'm the only one who's honest
About the truth I've yet to face in me
And everybody dies
Am I the only one who's nervous
Because nothing's going to save me

My dad took me to the funeral a few days later and I remember it was a perfect blue sky as we drove there, too, which just didn't seem right. I didn't even want to go, to be honest, since I was pretty scared, I guess, but it was kind of a good deal since I got out of school because of it.

The service was at this place called Green Acres, which was a stupid name, I thought, and Plan for Your Future … and Theirs is what they had on the sign out front, too. *Jesus.* But it was the first time I'd ever been to a graveyard and the way they had it set up so perfect really bothered me. I mean, with all the green grass and the trees and flowers all along the roads everywhere, while you're driving around looking for where your friend's going to be buried. It was the worst place I've ever been to in my life.

And I guess we took a wrong road at first and ended up at the back of the place somewhere, and when my dad turned the car around I could see a bunch of weird-looking buildings off to the side. Probably something to do with more people dying. But as we drove back along the fence and past the main building is when I could see all the cars along the road and a bunch of people there.

So we parked behind the last car and as we walked towards the service is when my dad told me how I could look at Dustin one last time if I wanted. And I couldn't believe he even said it, really, until we got a little closer and I could see there were other people doing it. And then Ms. Essary was there, standing right next to the casket, crying, since she was looking right at him, I guess. It was the sickest thing I could ever imagine, though, just standing there staring at my best friend when he was dead already. And my dad could see I was freaked out about it, too, so he told me I didn't have to do it after that.

The casket was set up next to a big pile of dirt from the grave, and they had a bunch of flowers around to make it look nice, I guess. And there was a huge eucalyptus tree nearby, too, which I thought Dustin would have liked.

And then we just watched everybody from a distance for a while, till I finally got up the nerve to go say I was sorry, at least. And Ms. Essary said thanks and gave me a hug, and so did Matt, come to think of it. And Dustin's dad even shook my hand, which was weird. I was glad I did it, though.

And then the preacher was there, so everybody got quiet and we all found a place to sit down on the white folding chairs they had set up in the grass out front. Me and my dad sat in the last row and when the preacher started talking, I got the weirdest feeling like Dustin was there somehow. I mean, like right there in the sun, in the empty seat next to us. He seemed glad it was over, too. And then we were just sitting there listening to what the preacher was saying about God and stuff, and it didn't seem so bad this time, really. And Dustin probably thought it was weird since the guy was talking about him a lot. And I felt a little better, I guess, knowing he was there, like he was letting me know everything was going to be alright in a way. Just like he did in the car that last time I saw him. But then he was just gone after that. And yeah, I was crying again, so what.

On the way home I told my dad about Dustin being there but I could tell he didn't believe me. I mean, he didn't say anything, he just got really quiet after that. And so I didn't say anything about him not saying anything, and it reminded me of that last game of chess me and Dustin played. Like me and my dad were playing some stupid backwards game then, too. Just say you don't believe me, Dad, I can take it. I still know he was there. Checkmate.

I was already feeling pretty different about everything at that point, though, so I didn't really care what anybody thought. All I knew was that I didn't want to do anything, or be friends with anyone, or even be around anybody after that. I mean, I just planned to stick to myself from then on and so that's what I did.

But then something weird happened, I guess, and since the older me was saying all that stuff about music before I should probably tell you.

It was a couple days after Dustin's funeral when my sister came by the house to try to cheer me up, so she took me to this movie called *Heroes*. It starred Henry Winkler, too, since he didn't want to be the Fonz anymore, I guess, and Sally Fields was in it, who I always had a crush on back then. But it was about this Vietnam vet who was trying to find his old military buddy after the war, only you found out at the end that the guy was dead the whole time, so the Fonz blocked it out, I think, since he probably had something to do with it. And it wasn't like the greatest movie I ever saw or anything, but it helped to know I wasn't the only one, maybe, since the guy had lost his friend, too, though.

Anyway, when the movie was over, this song started playing over the credits at the end, and I swear it was like somebody put the words and the music together to try to freak me out or something. And everybody was leaving and I knew we had to go, but I just stood there in the aisle and listened to it for as long as I could. Because everything the guy was singing was exactly how I was feeling, and the music that was going along with it made me feel it even stronger. But everything was just different when I heard that song, and I knew it was something I could count on, too, if I could just hear it again. And then I got lucky, I guess, since they were selling the soundtrack album out in the lobby before we left, and my sister ended up getting it for me since I begged her so much, and she felt bad for me, probably.

But I couldn't wait to get home so I could hear it again. I mean, I already had a record player, even though that was a piece of crap, too, pretty much. And I had some 45s from before that were kind of cool. Like the Doobie Brothers "Listen to the Music," and "Black Water" was on the other side, I think. And, "Brandi (You're a Fine Girl)" by Looking Glass was my favorite song from when I was a kid, and that Starland Vocal Band song "Afternoon Delight" was pretty good. And then Elton John and Kiki Dee's "Don't Go Breaking My Heart" was the last 45 I got, but I'm kind of embarrassed I even got that one now.

But none of those songs were anything like what I had just heard in the movie theater, and now I could hear it again, too. And that was the first album I ever got, so I didn't need to use the little yellow plastic 45 thingy anymore, either. And I remember the sound of the needle on the record when it first started, and "*CARRY ON MY WAYWARD SON*" is what the guy was singing really loud. And I could read on the back of the album that it was the name of the song, too. And I could see it was by the band Kansas, which sounded pretty stupid at first, but I didn't really care since the song was so awesome. But then I could see the song was from their album called *Leftoverture*, which sounded really cool right away, so I knew I had to get the whole album after that.

But just that one Kansas song on that *Heroes* soundtrack kept me going for days, especially that part when the guy comes in singing with the piano: "*And once I rose above the noise ...*" and I know you know the rest, but just that one part was the greatest, most beautiful thing I had ever heard.

And so that's when I just started walking around up along Camelback Road after school every day, or whenever I could, really, just walking and singing that song over and over in my head, until I ended up knowing it by heart, actually. And I didn't even want to ride my bike anymore, or my skateboard either, since it just felt right to be out there walking like that ... and I could see all the leaves in the trees really clear, and they were moving from the wind from the cars going by, and I just kept walking and singing that song over and over for some reason ... and maybe I was the one in the movie somehow, I thought, since I had just lost my friend and I didn't know what to do about it either ... And everything was still really sad, I mean, since Dustin was gone forever, but it felt like something new had started, too, maybe. Anyway, I know it sounds stupid, but that's just how I felt back then.

And then my brother came to the house a few days later and he was being pretty cool, I guess. But that's when he took me to the record store and helped me find that Kansas *Leftoverture* album I wanted so bad. And on the drive home, he even told me about some other bands I should listen to, but I can't remember who else he said. I mean, I knew he liked James Taylor a lot, and my dad did, too, since my brother *"turned him onto it.*" And that song "Fire and Rain" was pretty cool since it made me feel the same way, kind of. But Kansas was just different, though. I mean, just looking at the album cover on the way home was awesome. *LEFTOVERTURE*! But then my brother said some stuff as we pulled in the driveway, something about how Kansas was a complete rip-off of Yes, which really pissed me off, to be honest. So I almost yelled that Yes sucked shit again, but I stopped myself since I didn't want to get choked to death.

But I had the whole album then anyway, so I ran inside to play it and started listening for more songs that might be like the first one. And I could tell right away "The Wall" was awesome, too, but I pretty much learned every song on that record after that.

And then I started hearing even more songs on the radio that made me feel the same way, even though I never got the albums since they played them so much. But I remember waking up after it rained that one time, and hearing that Bob Seger song, "Night Moves," and I swear it was like he was right there with me, thinking about stuff, talking about the storm we both went through the night before.

And my sister had a bunch of cool albums that gave me the same type feeling, but I can't remember the names right now.

But that's pretty much it, though, anyway. And I know it sounds stupid, but I just walked around singing those Kansas songs to myself for like a year after that. And I didn't hang out or talk to anybody for that whole time, either, just like I said I would.

And I don't even remember when I started hanging out with Radick and those guys again, but I was tired of being by myself, I guess, and I knew people were saying stuff, too.

And we moved out here to the Junction not long after that, and they party just as much here, too, by the way. It's not like there's anything else to do, though, really. I mean, my sister gave me her old acoustic guitar, so I've been learning how to play a little, and some new friends of mine like playing too, I guess.

But the older me was just saying how it gets really bad after this, like I start drinking and doing drugs so much I almost end up like Pat or something. But we were thinking the same thing back when the cops were telling us Pat was dying, but then Dustin died instead, and he didn't even doing anything. *So I don't really give a shit*, or at least that's what Pat would say, anyway.

And I already told you about all the dream stuff with Dustin, and I probably said a bunch of other stuff I shouldn't have, but at least you know the truth now anyway.

Once Before

Here am I not equal to
 the will I might have had
Had I not have seen in you
 the place where I began
As helpless as the day you were born
 like a soul in the schoolyard
Where everything that's to become has
happened once before

And some will say that time is like a wheel
Turning around and around
Tomorrow it's all surreal
But time is a straight line against your will
Never again to be found, never again to feel

And you build your life
 on the graves of the forgotten
And you're justified
 by the things that they might have done

And a thousand years will pass by
 like one moment
and turn this wood to stone,
And everything that ever was
 has happened once before

And some will say that time is like a wheel
Turning around and around
Tomorrow it's all surreal
But time is a straight line against your will
Never again to be found,
 never again to feel

The soul, it lives through the body
Lives on tomorrow, lives on today

Here am I not equal to
 the will I might have had
And had I not have seen in you
 the place where I began

And some will say that time is like a wheel
Turning around and around
Tomorrow it's all surreal
But time is a straight line against your will
Never again to be found,
 never again to feel

Epilogue
April 28, 2015

Well, that was embarrassing. And remind me to never ask the younger version of myself what happened after that, either. But I'd really be an ass if I didn't correct a few things before I finish here.

To start: my brother never choked me like that, or that hard, anyway, or, even if he did, I probably deserved it. I mean, you heard the way I was back then. But there was never any *Yes is the best* beatdown, that I remember, anyway. And I even learned a few Steve Howe leads later on (the simpler ones, of course) after my brother gave me all his old Yes albums, since he ended up going techno punk with Barry Beam after that. But me and my brother are good friends now, so sorry I was such a smartass back then, Mike.

And it's funny how my sister Llory got off so easy through all this, when she was the one who hung me up on the Arcadia door handle by my underwear that one time. I mean, I probably deserved that, too, but it's just funny I never mentioned it.

But my sister's the one who played me all those great albums, like I said. And I know I couldn't remember all the names back then, but a lot of that stuff really stuck with me, Llor, so thanks. Like Karla Bonoff for one. I mean, her own stuff, mainly, but the songs she did for Linda Ronstadt were great, too. And J. D. Souther, and the Eagles, and Carole King, and Jackson Browne, and everything from David Bowie to Joni Mitchell to the Runaways to Bonnie Raitt made a lasting impression on me, for sure. Let alone, I never would have even started writing songs in the first place if it weren't for that first acoustic guitar you gave me. And then your old electric after that, and then that Black Strat with the hard case you gave me later on—the one I sold, like an idiot. I know—sorry, Llor.

And I really need to say something about my parents, too, since I'm sure I offended them somehow. So ... Mom. Dad. If you're out there listening somewhere, and maybe you're tapped into that ultimate, unified energy source Dustin was dreaming about, or even if you guys are just hanging out in my psyche as a reminder, and then we're all just space dust again after that ... Well, sorry I didn't have any fonder memories from back then. I mean, I was just kid, remember. I still love you guys, though.

And one last thing that's not even related to any family stuff, or to anything really, but I have to just say this: that I never bought that Elton John and Kiki Dee single either. I mean, I love all his other stuff with Bernie Taupin, but that was just some stupid pop song I heard all the time back then, so I don't know why I even mentioned it, really.

But besides all that, everything else is pretty much the way I remember it. I mean, it's hard to admit how scared I was, and selfish, and petty, and stupid … or ignorant, I guess. But at the same time, it's nice to be aware of it now so I can work on it, maybe.

And as for those songs that came to me recently, the ones that got me thinking about all this stuff with Dustin again in the first place. Well, I can't say I'm any closer to any real understanding after thinking back on all this, or how it's all connected from past to present, really. I just sense there's something meaningful there for me if I'm open to it. Like maybe the universe, and fate, and randomness, and destiny, and luck, and all the rest of it lined up for me on this one.

The Beginning.

So Be It

There's my lucky number
There's my favorite place
If only I were young
If only I were alive today

I would not be afraid
of the fire within
I could learn from my heart
and reinvent love again
To rise above and beyond
the way that it's always been
So I could rest in my soul
with the sun and the stars
So be it

There's my childhood corner
There's my mother's face
There's an open door
If only my past were alive today

Well I would not be afraid
of the voice within
I'd learn to question my faith
and reinvent God again
To rise above and beyond
the way that it's always been

So I could rest in my soul
 with the sun and the stars
So be it

For every moment I lost to the past
For every moment I thought would last
Now I have come here to start again
For every moment I've wasted

And now this day's before me
There's my sister's face
Recently she warned
Appreciate you're alive today

So I will not be afraid
 of the heart within
I'll learn to question my fate
 and reinvent my life again
To rise above and beyond
 the way that I've always been
So I can rest in my soul
 with the sun and the stars

www.ingramcontent.com/pod-product-compliance
Lightning Source LLC
Chambersburg PA
CBHW051946290426
44110CB00015B/2133